Ethical Virtuosity™

*Seven Steps
to Help You
Discover and Do
the Right Thing
at the Right Time*

Louie V. Larimer, J.D.

HRD Press, Inc. • Amherst • Massachusetts

ISBN 0-87425-767-0

Printed in Canada

Production services by Jean Miller
Editorial services by Suzanne Bay and Sally Farnham
Cover design by Eileen Klockars

• • • • •

Acknowledgments

My appreciation and gratitude are warmly extended to the following people:

- My son, David Gregory Larimer, and my daughter, Julie Ann Larimer, who by their simple being, daily struggles, and expressions of love remind me of my humanity and unique purpose in this life

- John M. Ventimiglia, whose financial support and personal encouragement made this work possible

- And all those people who, over the years, have participated in the ethics classes and leadership workshops I've conducted

There are many notions of what is ethical, but your discernment of right and wrong is what matters most.

Table of Contents

*To know what is right
and not do it is as bad
as doing wrong.*

*Ethics begins with
understanding yourself
and the way in which
you resolve ethical dilemmas.*

Begin the process of contemplation, and discover for yourself what you truly believe to be "the right thing."

Part I
Ethical Foundations

*It isn't easy to be
an ethical person.*

1 | *The Ethics Challenge*

A friend and I once planned a spontaneous January trip to Phoenix, Arizona to play golf, rest, and enjoy the warm climate for a few days. On our trip, however, we experienced some unexpected conditions and even grappled with an ethical dilemma.

It all began because I had two round-trip airline tickets from Colorado Springs to Phoenix that were going to expire by the end of January if I did not use them. So I invited my friend Dave to join me. He eagerly agreed. We made some calls to Phoenix-area resorts and found what we thought was a good golf package that included a double occupancy room, two rounds of golf, a cart, range balls, free drinks, and two free buffet breakfasts. We were quoted a figure that we thought was a bit pricey, but given our spontaneous desire to play golf and sit in the sun, we made reservations with the resort and were off to Phoenix the next day.

When Dave and I arrived at the resort, we signed in at the front desk, gave the clerk our credit cards, received the keys to our shared room, picked up our golf vouchers, and eagerly awaited the arrival of the following morning so that we could hit the course. We were like two children on Christmas Eve, anxiously awaiting Santa's arrival.

To our disappointment, the next day turned out to be rather cold, gray, and windy. Unfortunately, there was a frost delay on the golf course, and we had to wait several hours for the temperature to rise so that we could play. We kidded each other that we could have stayed in Colorado Springs and experienced the same weather for a lot less money! But we eventually got on the course and played in conditions that were, to say the least, not very good.

Just before leaving the course, we asked the attendant what the normal greens fees were, in case we wanted to return someday without the resort's golf package. To our surprise, the greens fees were fairly reasonable. As we drove back to the resort, we began to examine the "value" of our golf package, given the normal cost of the greens fees and our estimation of the cost of our room.

Both Dave and I travel extensively for our businesses and are familiar with normal and customary hotel charges for business class, single occupancy accommodations. We both agreed that our double occupancy room fell below the standards to which we were accustomed as business travelers. The more we looked at the value of the golf package, the more we began to feel that it, too, was not worth the money. Rather, it seemed an exorbitant and unfair trade practice of the resort, particularly given the poor playing conditions we had experienced that day.

Rather than dwell on this negative feeling, we resigned ourselves to our situation. After all, no one forced us to go to Phoenix, and we both freely chose to accept the pricing when it was given to us over the phone. Since Dave and I are both relatively upbeat, positive, and optimistic people, we simply resolved that the next day's golf experience in the warmth and sun of the Arizona desert would more than offset the unsettled feelings of our first day.

Call it misfortune, destiny, fate, or a cruel lesson in acceptance, but we awoke the next morning to the exact same type of cold, gray, windy weather we had experienced the day before. We were scheduled to play at a different golf course and had to fight the congested morning traffic of metropolitan Phoenix to get there. When we arrived at the course, there was no frost, but it was cold! We waited an hour, hoping for warmer weather. The sun taunted us by playing hide-and-seek in the clouds.

The morning finally got a little better, and we played our second day of golf, once again in conditions that were not what we had expected. When we finished our game, we asked the attendant what the regular price of a round of golf at the course was. The greens fee was almost double what we had been quoted the day before. Given this information, we felt a little better about the value of our golf package.

However, our analytical business minds could not resist re-calculating what we thought was our golf package's actual cost to the resort. Even with the higher greens fees for that day, neither Dave nor I felt that we had received a genuine golf value, which the resort had promised us over the phone.

Adding to our woes, Dave was suffering from the initial onset of the flu, and I had developed painful blisters on my left foot caused by a new pair of golf shoes. Further, it began to rain and neither of us felt like going out that night to experience the great dining pleasures Phoenix had to offer.

When we checked out the next morning, the clerk presented us with one bill, which seemed odd to me at the time since we had checked in separately. The price was exactly what I had been quoted on the phone. The only troubling aspect was that I thought that the quoted price was a per-person price, not a total price for two people. I was almost certain that I had confirmed that the quoted price was indeed a per-person price when I made the reservation.

I thought that perhaps the clerk had made a mistake, but my reservations about the value of the golf package crept into my mind, and I was delighted that the final bill made our golf package a pretty good value. Still, I was troubled. I had a feeling that a mistake had been made by the clerk in our favor, but I did not say anything at the time. Dave quickly gave the clerk his credit card and told her to put half of the charge on his card and the other half on mine. This she did without hesitation. We then went to enjoy our last free buffet breakfast before departing for the airport.

As we walked to the restaurant, we noticed that it was raining hard in Phoenix, the land of sun and desert. I felt uneasy and unsettled about the charges. Dave didn't feel the least bit concerned. He had not made the reservations and had not been privy to my conversation with the reservation clerk, and thought we had gotten a great value after all, particularly given the weather we had endured. Still, it bothered me that I had not spoken up and pointed out that the charge could not be right. I knew in my heart that if I had been overcharged, I would not have hesitated to point out the clerk's error. For some reason, I did not speak up when I was undercharged.

I mentioned all of this to Dave at breakfast, and we discussed what I should do. He easily picked up on my discomfort and noted the irony in the situation, given that I am an ethics and compliance consultant.

Indeed, I was in the midst of a personal ethical dilemma. The more I recalled my conversation with the reservation clerk, the more strongly I felt that the final bill was wrong and that the checkout clerk had erred in our favor. If so, the correct bill, by our calculations, would be exorbitant in light of the lower-than-business class accommodations we received, actual greens fee charges, and deplorable playing conditions.

During the remainder of our breakfast, I continued to be troubled by this incident and my own failure to press the issue with the checkout clerk. I couldn't help but recall a portion of a speech on ethics that I often deliver at conventions concerning personal choices. I was reminded of my observation that when you encounter or are confronted with an ethical dilemma, you have four choices.

The first is to ignore the dilemma and either act or refrain from acting as if there were no ethical issue involved. This choice generally results in conduct that is unethical or unlawful. I had done this at the checkout counter and didn't feel good about that choice. Since we had not yet left the resort, I still had the opportunity to deal with the dilemma and make it right.

The second choice is to comply with the law or some other established ethical prescription, requirement, or duty that specifically addresses the dilemma. This choice often results in what is considered by many to be ethical or honorable conduct. I gave this option some consideration, and decided that I had not broken any law—I simply paid the charges that had been presented to me by the clerk. I did feel that perhaps under the principles of contract law, I had made a legally enforceable promise to pay at the per-person quoted price. But then again, hadn't the resort waived the per-person price when it presented its final bill, which we paid? The option of following the law or fulfilling some prescribed duty wasn't of great solace to me.

The third choice is to consciously disregard the law and any applicable code of conduct, and act in an unlawful or unethical manner. Since the law didn't really apply to my dilemma on this particular day, this choice was not an option for me and my beliefs.

The fourth choice I have often urged others to consider is to act in a manner that exceeds the minimum requirements of the law and to engage in a more noble and virtuous course of action that reflects ethics, integrity, and responsible personal conduct. I was bothered that I had not done this at the time of checkout, but I still had time to go back and revisit the issue with the clerk.

As I finished my breakfast and discussed these options with Dave, I knew that I still had a choice to make. I really had two options. The first was to take advantage of what I believed was the clerk's error by ignoring the dilemma and rationalizing the mistake as some form of ethical justice in light of our perceptions that we had not received a good golf value. The second choice was for me to return to the front desk and bring my concerns to the clerk's attention.

I was still struggling with this issue and had not totally settled on a course of action when the checkout clerk appeared at our table to explain that she had made a mistake on our final bill. She asked if we would come to the front desk to rerun our credit cards to add the charges she had missed. She explained that they had lost one of the reservations and that the bill she gave us at our checkout was for a party of one, not two.

I was actually relieved that my dilemma had been resolved. Now I didn't have to make a choice. I didn't have to confront my inner feelings, weaknesses, and vulnerabilities. My dilemma was over. We paid the revised final bill without complaint. We made no mention of our feelings of disappointment. After all, we did have a choice as to whether or not to come to Phoenix after we were quoted a price.

As I reflect on my Phoenix golf experience, I continue to feel regret and disappointment in myself. I now know that I should have acted on my ethical instincts that something was wrong during checkout. I should have pursued the matter at the time the clerk gave me the bill, rather than agonize over it during breakfast. In retrospect, I like to think that I would not have left the resort without having the clerk recheck our bill to make sure she had not made an error in our favor. At least that's what I hope I would have done!

A Learning Experience

I learned a few things from this experience. I'm grateful for the opportunity it gave me to gain greater insight into myself. I've even made a few observations about how hard it is to do the right thing.

For example, the choice you make in any given ethical dilemma is a function of your personality, moral character, inner strength, personal core values, internal sense of what is right and wrong, moral courage, integrity, honor, and ethical fitness. These qualities are the result of several competing influences, such as your family, peers, friends, education, religious beliefs, culture, worldly experiences, the media, and even unconscious motivations and influences. The competing nature of these varied influences frequently makes choosing and following the right ethical and moral path a difficult task. Additionally, there are numerous temptations (e.g., ego, greed, lust, power, sex, etc.) and inner personal conflicts (e.g., self-interest versus concern for others, peer pressure versus individuality, truth versus loyalty, and conscious versus unconscious drives) that get in the way of doing the right thing.

In some cases, doing the right thing requires self-sacrifice for the betterment of others. In other cases, it requires taking an unpopular stand that subjects you to the criticism of others. Sometimes, the right or ethical thing to do is not even readily apparent to you. And in some situations, doing the right thing might be harmful to innocent bystanders.

The true, ethical, or moral path can become indiscernible because of the emotional context or circumstances of the dilemma. In some dilemmas, you are forced by circumstances beyond your control to choose between the lesser of two evils, thereby making a painful and hurtful choice. There are even occasions when you must choose between what appears to you to be two rights.

Doing the Right Thing

Indeed, doing the right thing is not as easy as simply talking or writing about it. Let's face it: Doing the right thing often requires a lot from us as human beings.

Unlike many scholars, philosophers, and professional ethicists, I don't profess to know what is right and wrong, nor do I have any particularly meaningful insights as to the moral principles by which you should live your life or conduct your business. I do know, however, from my personal experiences and reflections, that ethics, integrity, responsible personal conduct, and honor are important concepts to know, understand, and appreciate—and even more important, to incorporate into one's daily behavior.

Many great philosophers have observed that an individual's ethics are revealed and demonstrated by personal behavior and private conduct. I believe this to be true. I also believe that ethics, integrity, and responsible personal conduct can be taught. I believe that people can and will, under the right circumstances, change their behavior patterns and live more virtuous, caring, and loving lives.

At a personal level, this kind of change requires that you make a formal commitment to reflect and demonstrate ethics, integrity, and responsible personal conduct in all that you do. Specifically, this commitment requires that you consistently identify and resolve ethical dilemmas in a manner that reflects goodness and virtue. This concept is what I call "ethical virtuosity."

Ethical virtuosity is achieved by regularly engaging in and practicing seven specific steps: becoming self-aware, seeking ethical knowledge, developing an ethical belief system, practicing emotional discipline, consciously exercising your free will, demonstrating moral courage and personal accountability, and most importantly, immediately acting on your personal commitment to become ethically virtuous.

This book presents the seven steps that lead to ethical virtuosity. It also describes and explains several concepts that are fundamental to understanding personal ethical virtuosity.

At an organizational level, ethical virtuosity requires a genuine institutional commitment to follow twelve easy steps or strategies. If these strategies are implemented and followed by an organization's leadership, a highly ethical organization can be built and maintained. (These twelve principles are described in a forthcoming work entitled *The Twelve Principles of Integrity-Based Leadership*.)

The Purpose of this Book

The singular purpose of this work on ethical virtuosity is to motivate you to consciously reject unlawful and unethical conduct, and instead demonstrate ethics, integrity, responsible personal conduct, and honor as you face the daily challenges that life presents you.

I hope to do this by introducing you to some notable moral philosophies and principles; defining the nature of certain moral qualities or virtues; offering you a few of my personal observations and insights; sharing several ethical tools and concepts, helping you discover and explore your own ethical type, preferences, and core values; and challenging you to conduct your personal and business transactions in an ethical manner.

I offer my observations with a certain degree of trepidation. My concerns include the following:

- What do I really know about ethics, integrity, responsible personal conduct, and honor?

- What qualifies me to write about these principles?

- Am I any more ethical than my friends, colleagues, business associates, and competitors?

- What will others think about me after reading this work?

- Will people think I am a hypocrite and recall times when they thought I might have acted unethically?

- Am I just setting myself up for criticism by taking on this project?

I need to disclose to you that when I wrote this book, I was a lawyer. I know that for some of you, this automatically disqualifies me from having any credibility and knowledge of ethics. Yet my experiences as a trial lawyer have given me the opportunity to see, experience, and deal in a practical manner with the consequences of unethical decisions and conduct. Don't you think that most, if not all, lawsuits originate because someone did not act in accordance with the principles of honesty, integrity, commitment, and personal accountability?

Even so, what qualifies me to write about ethical virtuosity? Just because I've seen firsthand the devastating results of unethical conduct does not necessarily mean I am capable of providing you with any meaningful ethical insights.

I am the product of a traditional liberal arts education. Because of that, I have probably spent a bit more time than the average business executive thinking about abstract and esoteric notions of classical human thought and human experience. After all, what else can you do with a liberal arts education?

I attended a Jesuit graduate business school and took useful and practical courses such as Business and Society, Corporate Social Responsibility, and Business Policy. My fellow MBA students considered these courses to be soft, nontechnical electives. I think of them as lifesavers, since they were the only graduate courses I could really understand (I still struggle with the principles of ratio analysis and internal rates of return!).

Given this educational background, I had no choice but to teach or become a lawyer. I chose the safe, conservative route and did both! I convinced a few academic vice presidents that I could handle the rigors of teaching the required business ethics course *and* each mandatory course on business law. Hence, I've been privileged to teach ethics, law, leadership, and conflict resolution at several graduate business schools. In order to teach these courses, I was forced to read literature pertaining to business ethics. (As any good college professor knows, you have to stay at least one chapter ahead of your class—there is always one eager beaver who's out to test your knowledge!)

And so, it is from this limited perspective that I offer my insights and hope to give you something meaningful, practical, and personally relevant on ethics. Here is a sampling of the questions and issues that I will address in the pages that follow:

- What is **ethics?**
- What is **law?**
- How does law differ from ethics?
- What is **integrity?**
- What is **character?**
- Why are ethics and integrity important?
- What is **ethical virtuosity?**

- Where do ethical and moral beliefs originate, and how do they evolve?

- Why do people act unethically?

- What ethical principles do people actually use when confronted with a moral or ethical dilemma?

- What is a **core ethical value?**

- Why are core values important?

- What is **emotional discipline?**

- What is **reflective judgment?**

- What is **free will?**

- What is **moral courage?**

- How does one overcome temptation and the problem of human fallibility?

Before I reveal and share my observations and personal reflections, I want to challenge you at a personal level. Here are a few questions that only you can answer:

- Are you the kind of person who only pays lip service to the principles of ethics, integrity, personal accountability, and honor?

- Is your behavior and conduct consistent with your ethical talk?

- Do you truly have, and genuinely know, your own ethical standards and values?

- Have you acted in a questionable or unethical manner lately?

- Why did you do so?

- What, if anything, did you learn about yourself from that experience?

- Are you aware of any unethical, unlawful, or questionable conduct in your organization?

- What, if anything, did you do about it?

- Do you even care?

- How do you respond to a known ethical violation by a superior? By a subordinate? By a close friend or colleague?

- What do you think these responses reveal about your ethical "constitution"?

- Do you truly know which principles guide your decisions and behavior when you are confronted with an ethical dilemma?

- Can you look at your own conduct and articulate the internal principles that shaped your behavior in a given circumstance?

- Are you willing to honestly look at yourself from an ethical perspective?

- Do you know your core ethical values?

I encourage you to honestly reflect on these questions before reading further. Your answers to these questions will provide valuable insight into your own ethical constitution and give you a foundation for incorporating the concepts that are presented in the chapters that follow.

Finally, I want to emphasize that I offer my observations simply as a means of helping you discover for yourself certain ethical truths, knowledge, and insights that I believe you have buried deep within your soul, your conscience, and your heart. It is not my intention to teach you the absolute universal principles of ethics. You must discover these yourself. It is my clear intention, however, to help you discover or reconnect with them by getting you to commence a deliberate journey inward.

It is my hope that this book will become a catalyst in your continuing personal quest for self-discovery, self-exploration, self-mastery, and ethical achievement.

If you move in this direction, I guarantee that you will find many new insights and substantial personal rewards. As is the case with any personal journey inward, the extent to which you benefit is totally up to you. After all, I cannot teach you anything. I can only help you to discover it within yourself.

Ethics doesn't have to be abstract, esoteric, or complex.

2 | *What Is Ethics?*

Consider for a moment that your grandchild, son or daughter, niece or nephew, brother or sister, or close personal friend confides in you that he (or she) is in the midst of an ethical crisis. He says he absolutely does not know what to do, because he is torn between several conflicting interests and feelings.

Assume that this special person asks for your insight as to how he ought to go about resolving the dilemma. He tells you that he doesn't want you to tell him what to do, and he does not want you to tell him specifically what you think is right or wrong. He asks simply for your insight as to what "ethics" would require of him in his analysis and decision. He asks you to explain the meaning of ethics.

Would you be able to offer meaningful and helpful insights? What would you say? How would you respond to this precious moment?

Does the word *ethics* have a special meaning for you? Can you define it in a way that is simple, understandable, and meaningful so that even a young child can comprehend it? Do you know, at a personal level, what ethics really requires of you as a person?

A Beginning Definition

According to most dictionaries, *ethics* refers to generally accepted principles, judgments, or notions of what is right and wrong, good and evil, moral and immoral. The word is derived from the Greek word *ethos* meaning custom, practice, or usage.

Many people use the word *ethics* interchangeably with the word *moral*. In fact, several dictionaries list *moral* as a secondary definition for *ethics*.

Philosophers and scholars use the word *ethics* to refer to the systematic, disciplined study of or inquiry into what is right and wrong and, in some cases, into what ought to be considered as right or wrong. For these individuals, ethics is an organized compilation of judgments, principles, and concepts that define what is right and wrong and tell us how we ought to live our lives.

Five Levels of Ethics

There are five levels at which ethics can be discussed: personal, cultural, societal, professional, and organizational.

Personal Ethics

Personal ethics are judgments of right and wrong made by an individual. They consist of certain principles, values, and duties that a person believes ought to be the basis for personal conduct. Personal ethics are seldom, if ever, embodied in written form; they exist within your soul, your conscience, and your heart. They are reflected in your daily decisions, life choices, and personal conduct. Personal ethics vary considerably from person to person. A person who violates his personal code of ethics can—if he has a conscience or a personal sense of integrity—suffer anxiety, guilt, or remorse.

Aristotle tells us that a person's ethics are revealed not by one's speech, talk, or rhetoric, but rather by what one does on a daily basis and how one behaves. Buddha tells us that a person's true ethics are revealed during times of personal crisis, when surroundings, circumstances, and environment have become hostile or are no longer comfortable.

Many people innocently and mistakenly believe that they possess a well-thought-out and formal personal code of ethics by which they live. In my work, I often ask people to identify, articulate, and defend the ethical principles, values, and beliefs that govern, dictate, or influence their lives. When confronted with such an inquiry, most people pause, become somewhat reflective, and then offer a few superficial, abstract, and popular pronouncements that they believe constitute their ethical belief system.

In reality, most people don't take the time to consciously identify, contemplate, and choose their guiding ethical principles. Nonetheless, every person possesses a unique ethical belief system. At times, the underlying principles, values, and beliefs might not be readily or consciously apparent, resulting in personal conduct that lacks a clear articulated basis. Many personal ethical belief systems exist at an unconscious level, thereby resulting in choices and conduct that have no originating conscious basis.

Cultural Ethics

Cultural ethics are notions of right and wrong that are embraced by a particular ethnic or cultural group. These notions of right and wrong are seldom written, but rather exist in the minds and hearts of people who share a common cultural bond. The violation of a cultural ethic generally results in a judgment of disfavor or ostracism by the group against the individual who violated the cultural ethical norm.

I grew up in Hawaii—a genuine cosmopolitan melting pot of cultural diversity. Living within this unique island smorgasbord of culture, I witnessed and experienced the clash of cultural ethics almost daily. The following ethnic groups have a strong and vibrant presence in Hawaii: Native Hawaiians, other Pacific Islanders, Caucasians, Japanese, Chinese, Filipinos, and Portuguese. Each of these ethnic groups has distinctive views of what is right and wrong.

For example, the Hawaiian culture places a great value on love, openness, easy living, free-spiritedness, pleasure, and happiness. Time is of little importance to most ethnic Hawaiians. There is a principle in Hawaii known as "Hawaiian time." It refers to the custom of Hawaiians to show up for a business or work engagement or even a simple luncheon date

⬛

at a time that does not coincide with the agreed-upon scheduled time. I often jokingly remark to my Caucasian and Asian
friends that the only time Hawaiians are ever on time is for a
luau, party, or some other festive activity—provided that the
event doesn't interfere with whatever else is going on at that
moment!

The free-spiritedness of the Hawaiians and the cultural
value placed on easy living are in direct contrast with Asian
cultural notions of industriousness, attention to detail, hard
work, promptness, and duty over pleasure. As you might
imagine, these cultural notions of right and wrong often result
in a feeling that the "other" culture is wrong with respect to
the importance of time, work, and other aspects of life.

Most people in the United States have a significant cultural or ethnic bond. For example, each of us probably
describes ourselves as a member of (or heavily influenced by)
one of the many cultural groups that migrated to the United
States. Whether it be Italian, German, French, English,
Scandinavian, African, Spanish, Arabian, Jewish, or Asian,
each culture possesses a unique ethical belief system about
what is right and wrong. As a member of a cultural or ethnic
group, you are undoubtedly influenced in some way by distinctive cultural ethics.

Societal Ethics

Societal ethics are judgments of right and wrong possessed by
a distinctive society. Societal ethics are unwritten. They are
similar to cultural ethics, but apply to a grouping of people
that might include many diverse cultures. Societal ethics are
best understood, perhaps, by thinking in terms of working
classes and economic factors, rather than cultural or ethnic
characteristics.

In most U.S. communities, there are still clear-cut, highly
identifiable, and visible societal groupings. Individuals who
belong to exclusive-membership organizations such as country
clubs tend to hold notions of right and wrong behavior that

differ greatly from the notions of members of clubs and associations that are less restrictive and more inclusive.

I was raised in a working-class family, and I associated with other similarly situated families without the benefit of prestigious country clubs and "high class" events, such as debutante balls and symphony or ballet performances. I remember participating in and enjoying numerous social events and activities that most members of my current golf club would probably frown at or look upon with dismay. As a result of my early socialization, today I prefer—without hesitation—a good, boisterous, friendly, down-to-earth barbecue at a local park, followed by a visit to a carnival, over an evening of formality, elegance, and quiet beauty at the symphony or ballet.

I do not intend by these observations to promote societal or class differences and stereotypes; rather, I make these observations to illustrate that such differences still exist at a societal level and that they affect societal ethics.

Just as with the violation of a cultural ethical principle, the violation of a societal ethic generally results in social condemnation and ostracism.

Professional Ethics

Professional ethics are standards of conduct required of members of a particular profession, trade, or occupation, such as medicine, law, engineering, or accounting. These ethical standards of conduct have been developed by the profession and are regarded as the minimum expected behavior of members of the profession. These standards are written, codified, and widely distributed among its members. In essence, these professional ethics define the expected and acceptable behavior for the profession. Violating a professional ethic generally results in some form of professional discipline, including, but not limited to, admonition, probation, suspension, or expulsion from the professional group.

Today, almost every professional trade and occupational association has developed a professional code of ethics that governs its members.

Organizational Ethics

Organizational ethics are standards of behavior expected of people who work for an organization. You will find these standards reflected in value statements, organizational policies, and employee codes of conduct. In many organizations, the organizational ethics are not put in writing, but they can be discerned from the behavior of the top leadership. Violating an organizational ethic can result in ostracism and discipline.

Just as with personal ethics, organizational ethics vary considerably from organization to organization. Some organizations operate with little sense of business responsibility and no regard for how their conduct might affect others. Other organizations are highly ethical, demanding that the business conduct of their employees promotes and exemplifies certain highly regarded and noble virtues.

The Cause and Nature of Ethical Dilemmas

Ethical dilemmas often occur because a person's internal sense of right and wrong conflicts with a societal, cultural, professional, or organizational ethical norm or belief. Ethical conflicts also exist when certain personal notions of right and wrong conflict with each other.

There are times when justice conflicts with mercy, and there are times when a short-term gain conflicts with a long-range orientation. There are also occasions when an individual's interests conflict with the interests of a community, or truth conflicts with loyalty. Much of ethics is devoted to and focused on helping people resolve these conflicts.

When a person asks if a particular behavior is ethical, it is usually intended as an inquiry into whether or not the conduct is right or wrong. In many cases, the question is about which competing interest should take priority. For example, in a given circumstance, is justice more important than mercy? Should concern for others take precedence over self-interest? Is it more important that a person fulfill his duties, or is it more important to follow a conflicting intuitive sense or inner feeling? These are the types of questions that this discussion of ethics attempts to answer.

Developing a Personal Definition of Ethics

For some people, ethics isn't as abstract, esoteric, or complex as the scholars and academics make it out to be. For these folks, ethics is embodied in practical, applied notions of right and wrong. They understand ethics to be simple principles about how we ought to live our lives, treat one another, and balance profit, employee well-being, community, and personal self-interests.

These folks know and appreciate that their personal ethics are revealed

- In the character of the people with whom they do business.

- In how they conduct their personal business.

- In how they respond to trauma and critical disappointing occurrences in their lives.

- In how they act when no one is looking at them.

- In the daily choices they make.

- In their behavioral responses to the defining moments that occur in their lives.

Do you have a practical, meaningful definition of ethics? Can you articulate what ethics requires of you in any given circumstance? Can you respond in a helpful, insightful way to your grandchild, son or daughter, niece or nephew, or close friend if this person seeks your advice on what ethics means?

My Definition of Ethics

For me, ethics can be simplistically defined as *personal, freely chosen, and consciously adopted beliefs, principles, or notions of what is right and wrong, how I ought to live my life, and more importantly, how I should treat other people.*

Two important concepts should be recognized in my definition. The first is that ethics requires me to freely choose my beliefs and principles. This means that the beliefs and principles I choose must be uniquely mine, not imposed upon me by others. The second is that my choice must be the result of a deliberate, conscious decision; I must knowingly embrace the beliefs and principles that guide my life.

My personal concept of ethics also requires me to engage in conduct that exceeds or goes beyond the bare minimum requirements of the law and moves me closer to goodness and virtue. Thus, for me to be ethical, I must not simply conform my behavior to the minimum threshold requirements of the law; rather, I must engage in conduct that *exceeds* the law. I must act in a way that is virtuous and reflective of higher and more noble standards of right and wrong. My definition thus compels me to make decisions and engage in conduct that will move me closer to goodness and virtue in all that I do.

Implicit in this definition is that I must, at all times, comply with and obey all just laws. A *just law* is one that does not violate natural law or generally agreed-upon universal principles of right and wrong.

If a law is not just (e.g., the laws that for many years in the United States encouraged and tolerated slavery and, subsequently, racial discrimination), my personal concept of ethics requires me to disregard or ignore that law. In doing so, however, I must be willing and prepared to accept the natural and logical consequences of my disregard for the law.

Admittedly, this is easier said than done. When push comes to shove, I honestly don't know how I would respond in such a situation. I do know, however, that my personal definition of ethics would better prepare me to respond in a virtuous manner. This definition would give me guidance and, hopefully, inspire me to act virtuously and with honor.

Your Personal Definition

You need a personal definition of ethics if you are going to master the seven principles of ethical virtuosity. Your definition of ethics will serve as one of the fundamental building blocks upon which the seven principles of ethical virtuosity will rest.

Take the time now before reading further to discover and develop what ethics really means to you and what it requires of you as a person. Ask others for input. Discuss it openly with your loved ones. Challenge them to do the same. In doing so, you will acquire insight and a unique perspective for yourself.

*Laws are created
by humans as a means of
maintaining order in a society.*

3

What Is Law?

Is there a difference between ethics and law? As you might recall, my personal definition of ethics makes a clear distinction between law and ethics. This demarcation is easy for me as a lawyer. For those untrained in the legal formalities and philosophical underpinnings of the law, the distinction might not be so readily apparent or easily grasped. Consequently, a brief overview of the nature of law is presented as a means of helping you understand the differences between ethics and law.

Categories of Law

There are two major categories of law that must be pointed out in any legitimate discussion of the nature and meaning of law. The first is "natural" law and the second is "man-made" law.

Natural law is embodied in those universal principles of right and wrong that transcend and endure the tests of time, cultural biases, and historical forces. Natural law is God given and is discovered by study, contemplation, reasoning, and reflection. Natural law includes principles such as these:

- Murder is wrong.
- Children should be protected.
- Lying is wrong.
- Incest is wrong.

Natural law is similar to what I refer to as inherent, fundamental, ethical, or moral notions of right and wrong. As such, there isn't really much distinction between natural law, ethics, and morality.

In contrast, **man-made law** is the written expression of a recognized authority vested with the power to make rules that govern, control, and dictate the conduct of individuals and groups that make up a society. As such, man-made law is created by humans as a means of maintaining order in a society. Man-made law is voluntary in nature and exists solely by agreement of the people. The people of a society voluntarily relinquish to a recognized sovereign or authority the power to create rules for the betterment of the society as a whole.

Protagoras, a Greek philosopher, observed that the law is a voluntary agreement between members of a society that restrains individual rights, liberty, and behavior so as to maintain order and a civilized society.

In the United States, laws are made by four different types of authorities. The most commonly known law-making authority is the legislative body—a group of individuals elected by the people of a city, county, district, or state. The laws created by legislative bodies are generally referred to as "statutes."

Judges make law when they interpret statutes and declare or set forth rules they believe exist by virtue of the prior rulings of other judges. This type of law is known as "case" or "common" law.

The administrative and executive agencies of the federal government, as well as those of the 50 state governments, also make rules and regulations that have the force and effect of law. These administrative laws govern a variety of commercial activities such as safety, labor relations, food and drug processing, transportation, aviation, product safety, hazardous waste disposal, and truth and lending. The list of regulated activities is too voluminous to set forth in this modest treatment of the law. Suffice it to say that virtually every aspect of commercial activity has some federal or state agency that governs its conduct.

Law is sometimes made by the people through direct ballot initiatives, propositions, or referendums. These laws reflect pure democracy at work. Here, the law-making body comprises all people in a given jurisdiction who are entitled to vote.

Laws are enforced in several ways. The violation of some laws results in civil penalties, such as the payment of monetary damages to an injured or aggrieved party. The intent in such cases is to compensate the victim for the loss or harm caused by another's wrongful conduct. In other cases, the violation of a law can result in the imposition of criminal sanctions, such as a monetary fine, incarceration, or probation. In these cases, the intent is to punish the violator and deter others from engaging in similar illegal conduct.

Dual Nature of Law

By nature, law is both protective and restrictive. The Bill of Rights, for example, clearly is protective in nature, granting the individual citizen certain rights, such as freedom of speech and assembly, privacy, due process, and religious freedom. On the other hand, laws pertaining to zoning, land use, traffic, drugs, abortion, and gun control are viewed by many as deprivations and restrictions of individual liberty and freedom.

Naturally, a person's view as to whether a law is protective or restrictive depends on that person's particular circumstances, biases, prejudices, and prior experiences with the law. A corporate executive might believe the law is too restrictive with respect to business matters and too liberal when it comes to the treatment of criminals. On the other hand, a poor and underprivileged person might believe that the laws regulating businesses do not sufficiently restrict corporate greed and power and that criminal laws overly restrict personal expression and freedom.

It is important to your understanding of the differences between ethics and law that you recognize the inherent dual nature of the law and that you sort out the specific ways in which this duality is manifested in your behavior, thoughts, beliefs, and feelings concerning the nature of law.

It is also important to recognize that ethics is not law and law is not ethics. In some cases, the law might mirror personal, organizational, cultural, societal, or professional ethics. In many cases and circumstances, however, the law will not coincide with certain ethical standards.

Occasionally, people try to use the law to establish and impose a societal ethic. The Twenty-First Amendment to the U.S. Constitution, which for a time prohibited the manufacture, distribution, and sale of alcohol, is a historical example of the use of law to impose a societal ethic. The prolific number of United States Supreme Court decisions on pornography, abortion, sexual preference, and affirmative action are clear evidence of how far some people will go to impose their personal notions of right and wrong on others through the manipulation and use of the law.

As a practical matter and in most cases, however, law reflects minimum standards of civil behavior determined by an elected legislative body, by judges, and by administrative agencies. A violation of the law is punishable by a fine or imprisonment. As noted above, ethical violations result in significantly different sanctions (e.g., personal anxiety, guilt, social ostracism, embarrassment, public scorn).

Beyond Law

As outlined in the previous chapter, I believe that ethics requires behavior that exceeds and goes above and beyond the bare minimum requirements of the law. A good illustration of the distinction follows.

Assume that you are the parent of a 14-year-old girl who aspires to become a member of one of the U.S. Olympic teams. Your daughter has natural talent and above-average skills, but she needs additional work before she can achieve Olympic status.

She is invited to become a member of the U.S. National Junior Development Team, which is coached by a 36-year-old male who is highly regarded within the Olympic community.

Your daughter accepts the invitation and trains for several months with the team. She, and the other members of the team travel with the coach and are away from home for extended periods of time.

During one of her visits home, your daughter comments that the 36-year-old male coach is having sex with several of the older players on the team. Although the coach has not personally solicited or approached your daughter, she nevertheless expresses her concern and anxiety about the situation.

When you report the situation to the sport's governing body, an investigation is launched. The coach is open and candid about his affairs. He admits to having sex with several former and current players on the team, but asserts that the players were all over the age of 18 when the incidents occurred, and that each sexual relationship was consensual, voluntary, and without harm to the girls.

The coach asserts that because the girls were over the age of 18, his actions were legal, and that in the absence of any specific organizational policy or rule forbidding sex between coach and player, his actions were permissible. He insists that he be exonerated from any legal wrongdoing. Do you agree?

In most states, the law provides that the age at which a child becomes an adult is 18. As disturbing as it might seem, the coach's defense is legally correct. His conduct is legal, but it is not necessarily ethical.

Your Personal View of the Law

How do you perceive the law in this instance? Does it adequately protect your daughter and other young girls from the sexual advances of the coach? Should it do so?

What are your attitudes regarding the law? Do you believe laws are mostly protective of your civil rights, or are laws restrictive of your personal freedoms? Do you believe laws should mirror your personal ethics, or should laws reflect the personal ethics of others? Should laws be used to impose ethical notions of right and wrong on others?

Your personal answers to these questions will provide valuable clues and insights into your ethical make-up. Spend a few moments in contemplation of what your responses reveal about you.

Ask others to do the same. Seek out their perceptions of law in general and whether or not they believe there are differences between law and ethics. Listen and learn from their comments and observations. You might be surprised at how much you can gain from their individual and unique perspectives.

*Integrity involves
alignment of choices and conduct
that reflect who you are
at your inner core.*

*Integrity is the result
of living authentically.*

4

What Is Integrity?

In the ethics classes and training sessions I have conducted over the years, I have always challenged the participants to define the concept of integrity. When I've done this, there has generally been a short and often uncomfortable pause as the participants look at me with puzzlement, shift in their seats, and then divert their gazes away from me, fearing that if they make eye contact, I might call on one of them to share their personal insights. I always stand patiently as they reflect on and struggle with the difficult task of defining the salient characteristics and inherent nature of integrity.

What about you? Have you thought about integrity? Do you know what it really means? Do you know what it requires of you as a person? Do you have a definition of integrity that is meaningful, practical, and relevant?

Take a moment before reading further to jot down the initial thoughts and feelings that come to mind when you think of integrity.

Defining Integrity

Most of the students and seminar participants whom I've asked to define *integrity* have told me that integrity has something to do with "walking your talk," that it involves being "true to yourself," or that it means engaging in conduct that aligns with your inner beliefs, values, and principles.

When I began conducting ethics training, I thought that these formulations were pretty good. They were simple, easy to understand, helpful, meaningful, relevant, and practical.

Furthermore, the students and participants who came up with them genuinely liked their conceptions. They were proud of their ability to quickly and concisely capture the essence of integrity.

Upon deeper reflection, however, I realized that there are some notoriously unethical, immoral, and criminal characters who, under these definitions of integrity, would have to be classified as people of integrity. For example, didn't Adolph Hitler "walk his talk" concerning his inner views and beliefs about the Jewish people? Didn't Timothy McVeigh, the Oklahoma City bomber, act in a way that was "true to himself"? Doesn't the criminal behavior of the inner-city gang leader reflect and align with his inner beliefs, values, and principles?

This insight was unsettling to me. There was something disturbing about having to concede that unethical people like Hitler, McVeigh, and inner-city gang leaders had integrity. I did not want to spoil the nobility of the concept by allowing the immoral and criminal to be considered people of integrity. I no longer liked the definitions given me by my students and seminar participants. I felt that something was missing. I felt that the definition of integrity needed to exclude these undesirable miscreants from its virtuous glow. I felt that the characterization of Hitler, McVeigh, and gang leaders as people of integrity diminished integrity's inherent goodness.

In time, I turned to the dictionary for a rudimentary understanding and etiology of the word *integrity*.

I learned that integrity is a noun that refers to a quality or state or unimpaired condition of being sound, whole, complete, undivided. Some dictionaries even connect it to purity. I was reminded of the mathematical concept of the integer, which I remembered as being a natural or whole number. I discovered that some dictionaries include a secondary meaning for integrity, referring to it as the strict adherence to a moral code of values.

This information was interesting and somewhat helpful, but not satisfying in my quest for a better definition of integrity that took care of the Hitler, McVeigh, and inner-city gang leader problem.

My Definition of Integrity

I struggled for several years with this problem, trying to create a personally meaningful definition of integrity. I finally settled on a concept that I now offer to you as a model to consider in your discovery of what integrity means to you.

My definition of integrity now involves *knowing my deeper, inner, authentic self and consciously choosing to act in a manner that is consistent with my personal ethical beliefs, principles, and core ethical values.*

There are several individual elements of this definition. First, my concept of integrity incorporates and builds upon my definition of ethics. Remember that my personal definition of ethics requires me to behave in a manner that exceeds the bare minimum requirements of the law and moves me closer to goodness and virtue. This component easily takes care of the Hitler, McVeigh, and gang leader problem since their conduct does not conform to the law and does not reflect goodness and virtue. Thus, for me to be a person of integrity, I must do more than just "walk my talk." My beliefs and conduct must be inherently good and virtuous.

The second element is that if I am to be a person of integrity, I must have knowledge of my deeper, inner, authentic self. I must know who I am at my inner core. This knowledge must be unadulterated. I must, as Socrates implored, "know myself." This means knowledge and insight not only of my goodness and strengths, but also of my weaknesses.

At another level, self-knowledge also requires that I have insight into my ethical constitution and belief system. I must know what ethics means and requires of me. I must know which ethical principles are important to me. I must know the core ethical values that guide my life.

The next element of my definition is that I must make a conscious, deliberate choice to behave in a manner that is consistent with my ethical beliefs, principles, and core values.

In order for me to make such conscious choices, I must know, understand, appreciate, and control my inner drives, ambitions, motivations, passions, emotions, desires, ego, temptations, weaknesses, vulnerabilities, rationalizations, denials, unconscious preferences, and other hidden unknown influences—all of which, from time to time, obscure and prevent me from demonstrating, achieving, and living integrity.

I refer to the above items as "barriers to integrity," since they get in the way of being a person of integrity.

Each of us has his or her own unique and personal set of integrity barriers. Your integrity barriers are different from mine. But don't kid yourself: You do have them. It's part of your inherent human nature. The challenge for you, and for all of us, is to know that these barriers exist and to be able to identify them, understand how they operate, and master them by consciously choosing to disregard their negative influences.

Like most challenges in ethics, this is easier said than done. It is possible, however, once you have an understanding of what keeps you from being a person of integrity.

Moment by Moment

I often ask students and seminar participants whether or not integrity is an absolute. In other words, is integrity an inherent trait that a person either possesses or lacks? Is integrity like being pregnant? You either are or you are not pregnant! Likewise, can't it be said that you are either a person of integrity, or you are not?

What do you think? Is integrity an absolute? Are you a person of integrity? To what extent do you genuinely live out your ethical beliefs, principles, and values? Do these ethical notions move you closer to goodness and virtue? To what extent do others think you are a person of integrity?

I know that in my own life there have been times when I compromised my ethical beliefs, principles, and values and was not acting like a person of integrity. I also know that there have been times when I have genuinely lived out and demonstrated integrity. I suspect that you can say the same for yourself.

I have concluded that integrity, for me, is an aspiration. It is something I must strive for on a moment-by-moment basis. Each dilemma I face, each crisis I encounter, each situation in which I find myself presents an opportunity to move closer to becoming a person of integrity. It is during these daily moments that I am tested and given the opportunity to achieve integrity. Isn't the same thing true in your life?

Dr. Andrew Pipe, Chairman of the Canadian Center for The Advancement of Ethics in Sports, made an insightful observation at a conference at which he and I once spoke. He said: "The difference between what you say and what you do represents a loss of integrity."

In thinking about Dr. Pipe's observation, I offer the following modification: The difference between what you *say* are your ethical beliefs, principles, and values and what you actually *do* on a moment-by-moment basis represents a loss of integrity that can never be regained or replaced. You can only learn from these moment-by-moment losses and prepare for the next opportunity that is just around the corner. How you respond to these opportunities will determine the extent to which you achieve your integrity potential.

Your Definition of Integrity

If you want to prepare for the next opportunity for integrity, look back now on the initial thoughts you wrote down about integrity. Do those words feel adequate to you now, in light of what you have read so far? Can't you make a few enhancements to your initial concept of integrity? What does integrity now mean and require of you? What are your unique barriers to integrity?

*Character
is your moral personality.*

5

What Is Character?

Is there a person in your life—perhaps a family member, friend, colleague, boss, or subordinate—whose moral character you genuinely admire? Is there a historical, political, sports, community, spiritual, or other public figure you think of as having great moral character?

If so, reflect for a moment and try to identify what it is about that person that makes you think of him or her as a model of good character. What is it that sets that person apart from others? What one word best describes the essence of his or her character?

Do you know a person who lacks character? What is it about this person that is different from others? What distinguishes this individual from the person you regard as having character?

Your responses to this simple exercise should help you in defining and understanding the concept of character.

I have observed in my training sessions and in general discussions with leaders that many people use the word *character* in their conversations without much understanding of what it really means. Are you such a person? Can you honestly define and explain in a meaningful and relevant way to your son, daughter, or other family member what "character" means?

Defining Character

I confess that I had a hard time coming up with my own definition of character. For many years, I was one of those people who used the word, but never really thought much about what it meant. When I began to reflect on it, I realized how deficient my thinking had been.

As is my nature, I initially turned to the dictionary for help. I found that the word *character* refers to many things, including (but not limited to) a distinctive personal quality, mental and ethical traits, essential nature, notable traits, moral excellence, moral personality, and moral strength. Although I found these definitions helpful, I felt they were limited in helping me understand and discover something substantive and personally relevant about the concept of character.

After a period of patient contemplation, my thoughts and feelings on character slowly came forth from deep within my being. I share my concepts on character as a model for you to consider as you reflect upon what character means to you.

For me, character is a multi-dimensional concept that integrates my thoughts and feelings, conscious choices, free will, and personal behavior. Specifically, I define character as *the end result of one's thoughts and feelings, tempered by one's conscious choices (i.e., the exercise of free will), and manifested, revealed, and demonstrated by one's personal conduct and behavior.*

Life's Paradigm

This definition of character becomes clearer and more meaningful when you understand and appreciate what happens to you at a personal level as you live and experience the many challenging demands of life. As you move through life, you encounter unique human challenges, demands, obstacles, dilemmas, disappointments, excitements, highs, lows, traumas, situations, hardships, joys, and circumstances.

These life occurrences in turn trigger personal internalizations (i.e., inner processes and dynamics that happen deep within your heart, soul, mind, and psyche). These internalizations take many forms, including but not limited to intense emotions, feelings, attitudes, thoughts, reflexes, reactions, defenses, denials, projections, unconscious judgments, and preferences.

Internalizations happen automatically, quickly, and in an unknowing, unconscious manner. We encounter a situation, and then, before we are even consciously aware of what has happened, we experience one of the many internalizations that are possible.

How many times have you, for example, said or done something as the result of an intense emotional reaction, perhaps anger or fear, which you later regretted? Isn't it true that if you had simply thought more about it, you would have acted much differently?

When internalizations occur, it becomes imperative that they be tempered with sound, rational, logical, and conscious personal choices. If you fail to temper your internalizations, you will lose the opportunity to exercise your free will. You will remain a creature driven by emotional impulses, highly vulnerable to human weaknesses. By bringing to bear your capacity to reason, you will free yourself from your internalizations and create for yourself the opportunity to make personal conscious decisions that define who you are. Remember that all of your decisions are ultimately manifested, revealed, and demonstrated in how you conduct yourself and behave on a day-to-day basis.

This is what I refer to as "Life's Paradigm." The challenges of daily life trigger internalizations, providing you with the opportunity to define your character by your conscious choices and personal conduct.

Aristotle is known to have said that one's character is revealed not in one's speech, but in how one behaves. Buddha said that one's character is revealed not in times of comfort, but during times of inconvenience and hardship. Looking at your behavior, then, is the key to discovering your character.

I have found it helpful to think of my character as being a "metaphorical piece of art" that is in a state of constant creation and perpetual evolution toward an ideal expression of who and what I am. As the single artistic creator of my character, I alone paint or shape and mold my character. In a sense, my character is projected outwardly from deep within me by the choices I make and by my behavior. The outward or external projection of my character is perceived by those with whom I live, work, and play. Metaphorically speaking, it is within their hearts, minds, and souls that my character is artistically created or given meaning or expression. Their hearts, minds, and souls represent the canvas or artistic medium that gives my character life.

How Do You Define Character?

Please remember that my concept and definition of character is offered only as a model. I share it for the purpose of stimulating your personal contemplation of what character means to you. My definition works for me. It is relevant, helpful, and meaningful as I encounter and face the ethical dilemmas that life presents to me.

I encourage you to begin the process of reflecting on your concept of character. What does *character* mean to you?

The Character Continuum

Over the years, I have observed that people can be classified into common character "types." The first way of classifying character is along a continuum ranging from weak moral character to strong moral character. I refer to this as the "Character Continuum." Think of a scale from 1 to 10: 1 represents weak moral character, 10 represents strong moral character.

Weak moral character exists when ethical traits are not consistently demonstrated in a person's behavior. A person of weak moral character has a set of ethical principles, but the principles are not generally well defined. A person of weak moral character often succumbs to internalizations and other vulnerabilities. He stumbles in times of ethical discomfort, moral ambiguity, or when moral courage is needed.

Strong moral character exists when ethical traits are consistently reflected in a person's behavior. A person of strong moral character has a well-defined ethical constitution and rarely succumbs to internalizations and other vulnerabilities. He is firm and unwavering in times of ethical discomfort or moral ambiguity, or when moral courage is needed.

Where would you place yourself on the continuum of moral character? About average (at 5)? Closer to strong moral character? Closer to weak moral character?

More importantly, where would others place you on this continuum? How would others describe your personal character? What will others remember and say about your character at your death?

Because of certain human tendencies, we are often unable to accurately perceive ourselves. It is difficult to see ourselves as others see us. The essence of your personal character is probably somewhere between where you perceive yourself on the character continuum and where others would place you.

The Hierarchy of Personal Morality

Another way of looking at character is on the "Hierarchy of Personal Morality." This is a concept I created as a way to help people understand where their personal ethical journey has taken them and where their personal moral path can lead.

The hierarchy consists of five classifications of moral character. The five categories are Morally Corrupt, Ethically Challenged, Legally Compliant, Ethically Striving, and Authentically Virtuous.

A person who has a Morally Corrupt character, believe it or not, does have ethical beliefs, principles, and values. The Morally Corrupt person possesses strong notions of what is right and wrong. Unfortunately, these notions are not embraced by the vast majority of society. The Morally Corrupt individual embraces beliefs, principles, and values that generally result in socially reprehensible behavior such as criminality, violence, and deviant personal conduct that is abhorrent to society.

A person who has an Ethically Challenged character totally lacks any sense of right or wrong. It is as if the genetic material that is responsible for creating within a person an understanding of right and wrong is missing in the Ethically Challenged. This character type does not know what ethics is or what it requires. As such, the Ethically Challenged individual goes about his life completely oblivious to basic principles of morality.

Although the end behaviors of an Ethically Challenged person are similar to those of a Morally Corrupt person, there is a difference between these two character types. The Morally Corrupt person holds ethical beliefs that are intolerable to society. The Ethically Challenged individual does not even know it is possible to choose one's ethical beliefs, principles, and values. Hence, the Ethically Challenged person has no personal code of ethics to which he can hold himself personally accountable.

The next character classification is Legally Compliant. This term refers to an individual whose sense of right and wrong is derived from the bare minimum requirements of the law. The Legally Compliant individual makes no distinction between law and ethics. This person believes that a person has no duty, responsibility, or obligation other than to obey and comply with the law. The Legally Compliant person holds the belief that there is no higher, more noble standard of behavior. The Legally Compliant person equates ethics with the law. He believes that if it is legal, then it must be ethical.

Recall from Chapter 3 that this was the ethical view of the male coach who slept with several of his female players after they turned 18 years of age. The coach rationalized his behavior by stating that since the girls were 18, they were adults, and therefore, he had not done anything wrong. In other words, since he broke no law, he believed his conduct was ethical. This is reflective of a person who possesses a Legally Compliant character.

A person who has an Ethically Striving character is one who is aware that there is a difference between ethics and law, and strives to demonstrate higher, more noble, and virtuous principles in his daily conduct. The Ethically Striving person has a set of ethical principles, beliefs, and values that are highly virtuous. Furthermore, he genuinely wants to abide by and demonstrate these principles in his life.

The Ethically Striving person has traveled farther than many who are on the journey toward ethical perfection. However, the path is steep, and presents numerous challenges that often cause the Ethically Striving person to fall. Although this person might err from time to time, he will realize his mistakes, recover, and continue to strive for ethical achievement.

The final and ultimate character classification is what I call the Authentically Virtuous. A person who is Authentically Virtuous has a strong sense of right and wrong. His ethical beliefs, principles, and values are genuinely virtuous. He consistently lives them, demonstrating them in his decisions and conduct on a daily basis. The Authentically Virtuous rarely falters, and when he does, he holds himself accountable and accepts personal responsibility for his actions.

The most distinguishing aspect of the Authentically Virtuous is that others hold him in high regard. Others admire and hold him up as a model to be emulated.

The diagram on the following page depicts how the Hierarchy of Personal Morality looks. In my view, the three character classifications to the left of the solid line (Morally Corrupt, Ethically Challenged, and Legally Compliant) are unethical in nature, while those to the right of the line (Ethically Striving and Authentically Virtuous) are ethical and virtuous.

A Few Personal Questions

Where do you think you fall along the Hierarchy of Personal Morality? Morally Corrupt? I suspect not. Ethically Challenged? Possibly, but not likely. Legally Compliant? A possibility. Many people have shared with me that they fall into this category. Ethically Striving? I hope so! Authentically Virtuous? Maybe.

Where do you think others would place you? Would where you place yourself be consistent with where others place you?

Of greater importance, where in the hierarchy do you desire to be? Is being Authentically Virtuous a desire? Is it a possibility?

The Character Continuum and the Hierarchy of Personal Morality are not, by any means, the only two ways of looking at character. There are numerous other perspectives. I offer these concepts simply as a means of motivating you to examine your personal character. What is most important for your own evolution is that you take an honest look at yourself and begin to make changes in your character.

The Hierarchy of Personal Morality

Unethical	Ethical

Morally Corrupt   Ethically Challenged   Legally Compliant | Ethically Striving   Authentically Virtuous

*Some people naïvely believe that
ethics, integrity, and character
are not relevant
in our fast-paced, modern society.*

*You are what you do,
not what you say.*

6

Why Are Ethics, Integrity, and Character Important?

Are ethics, integrity, and character really important? Do these concepts make a difference in how you live your life, raise your family, conduct your personal business, and lead others at work? Is it possible that ethics is simply irrelevant, meaningless, and insignificant? Do ethical concepts add anything to the quality of a person's life? Does an emphasis on integrity contribute anything to how we interact and work with each other? Does character count in the commercial jungle and intense economic warfare characteristic of today's competitive corporate environment? Do ethical principles help you increase revenue, control expenses, make a profit, or maximize shareholder equity and return?

Some people believe that the answers to these questions depend on the life roles you are called upon to fulfill. There are those who believe that ethical considerations are a purely personal matter that should not be discussed or focused on outside the home and personal relationships. Do you agree?

Aren't there common elements that exist across the various important roles you play in your life? Aren't ethics, integrity, and character important in all your activities?

What are your primary roles in life? Spouse? Parent? Employee? Supervisor? Entrepreneur? Professional? Director or trustee of an organization? Chief executive officer? Public servant? Elected official? Educator? Community leader? Government official?

If you are married, do you want and expect integrity from your spouse? If you are a parent, do you want your children to learn and demonstrate high ethical standards? If you are a supervisor, business owner, or chief executive officer, are you better off if your employees and subordinates are ethical and bring integrity and character to their jobs, rather than leave these qualities at home? If you are a public servant, elected official, community leader, or director of an organization, is it true that those whom you serve expect you to perform your legal and fiduciary duties in an ethical manner?

The Importance of Ethics, Integrity, and Character at Work

Kouzes and Posner report in their seminal work, *The Leader-ship Challenge,* that most employees rank honesty as the most important leadership trait they want their bosses and leaders to possess. This insight is the most significant reason that ethics, integrity, and character are important. If you are to become a more effective leader, you must integrate ethical principles into your daily leadership behaviors.

Clearly, ethics, integrity, and character are important and relevant on a personal level. They give meaning and add quality and value to our relationships. The adverse, hostile environment in which we conduct business provides another important reason why ethics is vitally important. Consider the following:

Litigation is at an all-time high. Juries now routinely return multimillion-dollar verdicts. The financial, legal, and personal consequences of employee misconduct, internal fraud, scandal, corruption, and litigation are so devastating that failure to take aggressive, proactive, and preventative measures can result in multimillion-dollar judgments, bankruptcy, outrageous attorney fees, loss of public confidence, decline in employee morale, loss of customer loyalty, tarnished reputations, and destroyed careers.

It doesn't have to be that way. Ethics, integrity, and character can prevent and deter unlawful and unethical conduct. Don't deceive yourself: The business and legal environment in which your organization operates is not friendly. It is a hostile and unforgiving climate. Consider the following real-life examples as evidence of this madness.

Citigroup. In 2003, the nation's number-one financial services group agreed to pay $240 million to settle predatory lending charges in the largest consumer-protection settlement in the history of the Federal Trade Commission.

Enron. Under the supervision of CFO Andrew Fastow (and with approval from the board and auditor Arthur Anderson), Enron established "off-the-books" entities to hide company debt. Hiding the debt increased Enron's paper profits and boosted the stock. When the stock fell, Enron was forced to reveal its hidden partnerships and then everything disintegrated.

HealthSouth. In 2003, five former HealthSouth executives were sentenced for their roles in the organization's $2.7 billion accounting scandal. The five sentences were the first to be handed down to 15 former HealthSouth executives who pleaded guilty to fraud. All 15 agreed to cooperate with the government against former HealthSouth CEO Richard Scrushy, who was accused of defrauding the government and investors by directing the health care accounting fraud.

Arthur Anderson, LLP. On June 15, 2002, a jury found this accounting firm guilty of obstructing justice when it shredded Enron documents. Its involvement with questionable auditing practices caused the organization's demise; partners lost millions of dollars, the 26,000 employees lost their jobs, and the $4.5 billion enterprise collapsed.

WorldCom. At the direction of its CFO, Scott Sullivan, WorldCom counted $4.8 billion in ordinary operating costs as capital expenses in 2001 and 2002, allowing the company to report profits when it actually lost money.

Savings and Loan Fraud. In 1995, the Department of Justice reported that 5,506 former savings and loan officers, directors, CEOs, attorneys, accountants, and consultants were convicted of fraud in connection with a major savings and loan fiasco. Of the 5,506 people convicted, 4,157 were sentenced to prison. Courts imposed fines of $45 million and ordered restitution of $2.9 billion.

Ford Motor Company. In 1995, a jury awarded $62.4 million to two women injured in a Ford Bronco II rollover; $58 million was awarded in punitive damages, based on evidence that Ford allegedly hid evidence of the vehicle's deficiencies.

Phar-Mor. In 1995, Michael Monus, former president of Phar-Mor drug chain, was convicted of 109 counts of fraud.

United Way of America. In 1995, William Aramony, former president of United Way of America, was convicted in federal court of fraud and misappropriation. This was preceded by reports of Aramony's nepotism and excessive spending of donated dollars for first-class travel, private limousines, and other luxury items or services.

Federal Government. In 1994 and 1995, the federal government spent $32.6 million on five independent-counsel probes into ethics and law violations by a variety of government officials.

University of Miami. In 1995, the NCAA imposed sanctions against the Miami Hurricanes that cost the University of Miami a football bowl appearance and a reduction of at least five scholarships each season through 1997. Additionally, Miami was placed on probation for three years and was required to forfeit 13 new football scholarships for the '96–'97 season and 11 for the '97–'98 season.

Prudential Insurance Company. In 1996, it was reported that Prudential might be forced to pay up to $1 billion to resolve accusations of abusive sales practices on the part of its insurance representatives. Press reports indicated that Prudential offered $2 billion to settle claims against it.

Philadelphia Police Department. In 1996, ten lawyers and ten support staff were hired to work full-time to prepare a defense for the City of Philadelphia in a series of lawsuits associated with police fraud and scandal.

Texaco. Texaco was embarrassed by a racial discrimination lawsuit several years ago when certain high-level officers were taped making racially disparaging comments and discussing the possible destruction of incriminating evidence. Texaco settled the claims by agreeing to pay $174 million.

State Farm Insurance. In 1996, a Utah jury returned a $147 million verdict against State Farm after hearing evidence of fraudulent and deceptive business practices.

The cases cited above are not isolated examples. Although they are noteworthy, they represent only the tip of the iceberg. Every day, in courtrooms all across America, similar verdicts are rendered against organizations resulting from the absence of ethical principles, organizational integrity, and character. A more significant fact is that an unknown number of lawsuits are settled every day in order to avoid the adverse publicity that would result from public disclosure of wrongful conduct.

Some people naïvely think that employee misconduct, fraud, scandal, corruption, and litigation are not genuine threats to their organizations. These people mistakenly believe that they are somehow immune, and that they and their organizations are not at risk. This belief is not reasonable: A simple review of major litigation in the United States indicates that many reputable organizations and executives have indeed suffered the embarrassing and debilitating effects of fraud, scandal, corruption, and litigation—the results of an absence of ethics, integrity, and character.

Don't be a victim of your own self-deception. The threat is real. As the leader of your organization, department, or work unit, you are at risk if ethics, integrity, and character are not top priorities. Just remember, any one of your employees could easily cause you to become an unwitting victim of misconduct.

Ethics, integrity, and character are also relevant if you want to

- **Demonstrate and reflect your personal commitment to** and expectation of **ethical behavior.**

- **Promote and encourage** sound ethical decisions and responsible behavior.

- **Prevent litigation** and the waste of time, effort, energy, and money on ill-advised lawsuits.

- **Preserve the public's confidence** in your organization, your products, and your services.

- **Provide an organizational conscience** that helps employees to responsibly face and overcome the ethical challenges they will encounter in your service.

- **Improve employee morale** by strengthening your organization's relationship with its employees.

- **Provide a framework** for understanding that ethical dilemmas can and should be confronted and resolved in a thoughtful and meaningful manner.

- **Save your money** for years to come.

- **Protect your profitability** and preserve your bottom line.

- **Reduce the threat** of employee misconduct, fraud, scandal, corruption, and litigation.

If you believe ethics, integrity, and character are not relevant to you and your organization, you are vulnerable to the following consequences:

- Loss of your job and your career

- A tarnished reputation

- Multimillion-dollar judgments against you

- Having to pay outrageous attorney fees

- Loss of the public's confidence in you and your organization

- Loss of customer loyalty

- Adverse publicity, embarrassment, and humiliation

- Declining profits, diminished shareholder returns, and loss of equity

A Few Personal Questions

What do you think about ethics, integrity, and character? Are they important, relevant, and meaningful concepts for you?

*Ethical knowledge and insight
can help you make better decisions,
but doing the right thing
is fundamentally a
matter of personal choice.*

7

Can Ethics Be Taught?

One of the controversies that exists in the academic and professional worlds is the question of whether or not ethics can be taught. There is little dispute that ethics can and should be taught to children by their parents. There is disagreement, however, as to whether ethics can or should be taught in settings outside the home.

In almost every ethics class or training session I have taught, there has always been at least one student who insisted that the ethics class was meaningless and a total waste of tuition and time. I've also had discussions with a small number of business executives who maintain that ethics training makes little or no difference in the bottom-line performance of an adult employee.

The rationale for these views is that the adult employee or student has an unchangeable ethical belief system or character that cannot be influenced by any ethical knowledge acquired during adulthood. Those who hold this view believe that a person's character is set in stone during childhood, and that an ethics class or a mandatory ethics training module is simply "too little, too late." The view does not dispute that ethical knowledge can be taught or transferred. It simply says that teaching ethics does not make a difference in the lives or conduct of people.

This represents a rather narrow and pessimistic view of human potential. It disregards the fact that human beings have free will—the uniquely human ability to choose how to respond to difficult situations and circumstances.

Because you have free will, you possess the ability to make conscious choices as to how you will behave. If this were not so, your human behavior would be nothing but a series of hopelessly unchangeable, conditioned reflexes emanating from your childhood experiences.

This is not to say that your developmental history is an insignificant factor in how you behave in a given situation. Your childhood experiences with family, friends, school, and religion do indeed influence your behavior and emotions. They do not, however, cause a total shut-down of your human autonomy or free will.

The experiences of Victor Frankl and other Holocaust survivors illustrate the enduring quality of human free will and the resilient ability of humans to choose dignity and life in a situation of human depravity. It is this same human quality that allows you to choose enlightened and responsible behaviors as an adult.

Furthermore, your intellectual, emotional, moral, and spiritual components are constantly evolving. They change in response to new knowledge and worldly experience. You need only look at your own life and experiences to see the growth and changes that occur. Consequently, teaching ethical knowledge, principles, concepts, belief systems, decision-making models, and analytical techniques can influence this natural process of individual human evolution and growth.

Granted, teaching someone about ethics might not necessarily cause that person to act more ethically. The knowledge will, however, help the student recognize, understand, and appreciate that all ethical dilemmas present options and choices, some of which are more noble and desirable than others. Ethical knowledge will give an individual a better framework from which to analyze an ethical dilemma and consciously choose a path that will lead to a virtuous solution.

Some people believe that ethics, integrity, and character cannot be taught because they unconsciously fear that the ethics curriculum will challenge their fundamental beliefs of right and wrong, or impose upon them a specific ethical view or perspective. I must caution you that there are many ethicists who try to do this very thing. They self-righteously believe they have found the essence of ethical truth and knowledge, and they try to impose their perspectives on others. This is not what teaching ethics ought to be about. In my view, when you teach ethics, you are helping people make informed, conscious decisions to move closer to goodness and virtue.

The teaching of ethics is much like the teaching of music; the essential foundations, theories, principles, and techniques can be taught. It is up to the student, however, to use that knowledge of music theory to create music rather than noise. Likewise, the teaching of ethical knowledge can result in either virtuous or unethical behavior. Clearly, the choice to act ethically is entirely up to the individual.

*The decision you make
when confronted with
an ethical dilemma is
a function of many factors.*

8

Where Do Ethical Beliefs Originate?

Do you have an opinion about any of the following controversial topics?

- Abortion
- Capital punishment
- Gun control
- School prayer
- Physician-assisted suicide
- Gay rights

I suspect that you have a strong opinion about each one of these issues. Choose the one issue about which you feel most strongly. Put the topic firmly and squarely in your mind.

What is your opinion on the issue you have chosen? Do you favor it? Do you oppose it? What are your feelings concerning how this issue ought to be resolved?

More importantly, can you identify the origin of your beliefs and judgment concerning the issue you have selected? In other words, where does your belief on the chosen topic come from? What factors have influenced and determined your judgment?

Influences on Ethical Beliefs

There are several factors that affect how you feel about a controversial issue or ethical dilemma. These factors probably include parental upbringing, religious or spiritual teachings, peer pressure, education, role models, cultural influences, societal pressures, law, the media, and your worldly experiences. Are you aware of the extent to which each of these factors has contributed to your ethical judgments of what is right and wrong?

Most people report that their parents have had an important influence in how they resolve ethical dilemmas. Sometimes a person discovers that he has become very much like his parents when it comes to ethical values, principles, and beliefs. Although it might not seem likely during adolescence and early adulthood, it is not uncommon for a person to ultimately adopt and hold ethical views and opinions that are remarkably similar to those of his parents.

In many cases, there is no similarity. There is overt disagreement. In these cases, the parental influence has been to drive the child to adopt and hold beliefs vastly different from the parent in an attempt to achieve individuation and differentiation. Nonetheless, the parent has contributed to the child's adult judgments.

Religious and spiritual teachings might also influence how you resolve ethical dilemmas. Because of the inherent judgments of morality contained in religious doctrine, your religious experiences tend to have a profound influence on your ethical responses and choices when you are confronted with an ethical dilemma.

Likewise, your educational background and experiences affect how you resolve ethical dilemmas. More often than not, a military academy graduate thinks and feels differently than a liberal arts college graduate. A business major approaches ethical dilemmas differently than does an art or music major. A person with no college education will most likely have an even more diverse approach and value system. Each of these academic backgrounds values different principles, thoughts, and feelings concerning what is important in life and how one ought to treat other people. In essence, education provides the opportunity for unique and diverse insights that might not otherwise be readily available.

Peer pressure is another influence that must be recognized. There is a natural human tendency to want to be accepted and admired by one's peers. This proclivity is particularly strong during adolescence. In many cases, a person carries this tendency well into adulthood. It is expressed in many subtle ways, such as wanting to have the right car, belonging to the right social or country club, buying the latest clothing fashions, sending your children to acceptable schools, or socializing with the right people. It is not surprising that in many ethical dilemmas, people will conform their choices and behavior to those most acceptable to their peer group.

Violence and the use of coarse language in the media, as well as the way the media characterizes or portrays sex, love, marriage, and divorce, also contributes to how you think about and view the ethical dilemmas you encounter. Television and movie productions have had a subtle but profound influence on how people think and feel about certain life situations and personal behavior.

Your personal experiences also shape and determine how you resolve ethical dilemmas. An individual who has been the victim of a heinous crime most likely has views about the death penalty and gun control that are different from those of a liberal college professor. A person who has watched a loved one suffer the unmerciful and painful affects of a terminal disease that takes away the individual's humanity and dignity most likely has intense feelings about physician-assisted suicide—particularly when the loved one stated his or her preference for a dignified end.

The influences that affect your ethical preferences and choices are numerous. They occur consciously and unconsciously. The unconscious influences are also known as our *internalizations,* discussed in Chapter 5.

Conditioned Reflexes and
Reflective Judgment

There are two other sources of ethical beliefs that I haven't discussed yet, but that are of great importance. They are conditioned reflexes and reflective judgment.

Conditioned reflexes are the end result of your personal internalizations described in Chapter 5. They are your unthinking behavioral responses to the ethical challenges, demands, and circumstances you encounter. They are automatically triggered by certain hot spots and vulnerabilities that result from your prior experiences. Everyone experiences conditioned reflexes. They happen frequently and occur unconsciously. But with practice, insight, understanding, and emotional discipline, you can minimize and even control your conditioned reflexes.

The biggest challenge is to become aware of your conditioned reflexes as they occur. Can you identify when you experienced an unthinking, conditioned reflex? What was the trigger? What was the emotional hot spot that set you off? Do any of your ethical judgments pertaining to abortion, capital punishment, gun control, school prayer, physician-assisted suicide, or gay rights result from a conditioned reflex?

Reflective judgment is another source of ethical beliefs. *Reflective judgment* is a disciplined, deliberate process of pausing, reasoning, and weighing the alternatives and sorting out various internalizations and conditioned reflexes in order to engage in rational thinking and judgment before acting. Most of us don't do enough reflective judgment, if any at all.

To achieve ethical virtuosity, you must be able to identify the dominant ethical influences in your life. Do they include family? Peers? Education? Media? Worldly experience? Religious teachings? Conditioned reflexes? Reflective judgment? Answering this question will help you become aware of your individual influences, understand how they affect your choices, and put them into perspective by engaging in reflective judgment.

On occasion,
even good people
do stupid things.

*Be not a prisoner of
your thoughts, nor a slave
of your emotions.*

9

Why Do People Act Unethically?

Have you ever wondered why people engage in unethical conduct? Are you aware of why you have acted unethically in the past? Here is a true story that might help you find answers to these questions.

Members of a small church made arrangements with a bowling alley for the church to start a bowling league for its members. The bowling alley proprietor and the church members verbally agreed to the arrangements. No written agreement was signed.

A few days before the church's bowling league was to start the first games, the proprietor notified the church that it could not use the alley on the agreed upon day and time. The reasons given were that the proprietor could rent the bowling lanes promised to the church to a much larger group for a longer period of time, and that the larger group would be heavy consumers of food and drink, whereas the church group would not. The proprietor admitted that he had promised the lanes to the church, but he nonetheless breached his promise to the church and refused to honor his commitment.

Do you believe the bowling alley proprietor acted unethically in refusing to honor his promise to the church? I suspect that you will agree with me that the proprietor acted in an unethical, unfair, and dishonest manner. Most people hold to the principle that promises and commitments to customers and clients should be kept, and that a subsequent opportunity for additional profit does not justify the failure to keep a prior commitment or promise.

After hearing of this occurrence and concluding that the proprietor was unethical in his behavior, I became intrigued by several other questions.

Specifically, I wondered what motivated the proprietor to act in such a manner. What was his thought process as he canceled the church's arrangements? What went on inside his mind, heart, and soul as he broke his promise to the church? Was the motivation greed? Financial necessity? Ignorance? Did the proprietor believe that the consequences of breaching his promise would be nominal? Did he think that his behavior was justified by the increased profit derived from the larger group?

You and I will never know the specific thoughts of this proprietor. I briefly considered calling and asking him to share with me the rationale for his decision. Fortunately, common sense overcame my impetuous curiosity, and I wisely chose to reflect instead on the safer, deeper, and more general question of why people engage in unethical conduct. The following observations emerged from this process.

Ignorance

Some people are genuinely ignorant of what is right and wrong in business conduct. Incredibly, these people do not know what is ethically expected of them in certain situations. This results from a variety of factors, including but not limited to absence of a sense of right and wrong; lack of a personal conscience; character deficiency; no positive role model; absence of an applicable code of ethics; failure to know of the existence of an appropriate code of conduct; failure of the code to address the specific issue; and failure of an organization or trade association to develop and/or clearly communicate a standard of ethical behavior.

No One Will Find Out

Some people are aware that a particular course of conduct is unethical, but they consciously choose to engage in wrongful behavior because they believe that no one will ever learn of it. The notion here is that if you can get away with it, you might as well do it.

The Ends Justify the Means

Many intelligent people faced with a difficult choice or decision compare the end result they hope to achieve to the harm that will occur if they act unethically in order to achieve it. In this deliberation, they will choose the course of action that will accomplish their desires, regardless of the harmful consequences that will occur if their unethical actions are exposed. People who use this rationalization often explain that their unethical conduct "was a necessary evil" in order to achieve their end result.

Inexplicably, unethical conduct has sometimes resulted from the notion that an ethical standard can and should be breached in order to advance or promote a higher or more noble cause or principle. This was the rationalization of those involved in the Watergate and Iran-Contra controversies—the overriding, driving force of the Watergate conspirators and the Iran Contra operatives, who engaged in unlawful, unethical conduct in a vain, desperate, and misguided effort to advance what they believed were critical national interests and policies.

Nominal Consequences

Some people are aware that a particular behavior is unethical, but consciously choose to engage in the wrongful conduct anyway, assuming that the consequences will be minimal. The perception here is that being caught will not be harmful. The nominal-consequences belief is a variation of the ends-justify-the-means rationalization. It differs from the ends-justify-the-means concept in that the expected consequences are perceived as being nominal and not likely to occur.

Others Do It

Sometimes, unethical conduct is justified by the notion that *Others are doing it, so it really can't be that bad,* or *If I don't do it, I'll lose a competitive advantage in the marketplace.*

This belief is a primary reason why we are witnessing and experiencing predatory and deceptive trade practices. It is also the reason why many of our athletes have turned to performance-enhancing drugs: They perceive that their competitors are using these substances, and they don't believe they can remain competitive unless they create a level playing field by also getting the advantages such drugs afford.

Prior or Current Perceived Unjust Harm

There are occasions when people believe they are victims of a prior or current unjust harm, and that this unfair treatment justifies their own unethical conduct. This is akin to the notion of balancing or evening out the playing field. I've had students, business executives, and seminar participants readily admit that because they felt underpaid or otherwise mistreated by a boss or supervisor, they intentionally padded an expense account as a means of obtaining just compensation.

The most drastic and extreme form of this belief is the increasing frequency of workplace violence that is now occurring. Employees who feel that they have been unjustly treated are seeking what they believe is justified revenge by committing acts of violence at work.

Unrealistic Demands and Pressure

Unethical conduct is often caused by employers who place unrealistic demands or pressures on employees who are unable to meet such impossible deadlines or performance standards.

Such pressures encourage and tempt employees to bend the rules in order to avoid the harsh consequences of failing to meet a deadline or standard. In these circumstances, the perception is that the consequence of not meeting the deadline or business goal is far greater than the harm suffered from the unethical conduct. Hence, it seems better to go along with the unethical conduct than to take the risk of losing one's job.

Financial Necessity

Unethical conduct is sometimes motivated by the threat of economic or financial disaster. People occasionally find themselves financially strapped and in need of money that they cannot obtain in a lawful or legitimate manner. Consequently, they seek other means of meeting their basic economic needs.

Low-paid law enforcement officers working incredibly long hours in a high-risk job are particularly vulnerable to such pressures. The belief is that a little unethical conduct is nothing, compared to the personal need for money in order to survive. Many small-scale embezzlers have admitted that a personal financial crisis, coupled with opportunity, was the major reason they stole from their organizations.

Egoism

Egoism refers to self-centered decision-making and conduct without regard for other people. Often, unethical conduct results from a person's failure to accommodate or consider the needs of other people. When this is coupled with a tendency to avoid personal accountability for one's actions, unethical and wrongful conduct is inevitable.

It's Not Illegal

Some people believe that as long as a certain conduct is not prohibited or banned by law, it is permissible to engage in that conduct. This was the rationale of the sports development coach discussed in Chapter 3 who believed it was entirely acceptable to have sex with his female players, as long as they were 18 years of age. It is also the rationale of the legalized houses of prostitution in Nevada and the tobacco companies who continue to exploit the addictive aspects of cigarettes.

Just This One Time

There are times when you *know* certain personal conduct is wrong, but you do it anyway under a mistaken belief that you are only going to do it this one time and you will never again engage in such conduct. A leading potato-chip manufacturer says in its television commercials that once you've tasted the chips, you won't be able to eat just one—you'll want the whole bag. This is the problem with the just-this-one-time rationalization for unethical conduct: As many of us have learned the hard way, once you've started down a path of misconduct, it is extraordinarily difficult to stop. There is rarely just one occurrence of misconduct. A prime example: Have you ever told a lie and then had to lie to others in order to protect and preserve the first lie?

Peer Pressure

The need for acceptance makes us all vulnerable. During our teen years, we were subjected to strong peer pressure to comply with and abide by certain perceptions and expectations. Thinking back on those times, didn't you cave in to peer pressure? The need to be liked and accepted never goes away; it might diminish as we individuate and develop greater confidence in ourselves, but the pressure to conform never dies. Peer pressure is often used in the corporate world as a means to motivate an individual. Have you ever been in a situation where you knew you were right, but compromised or complied with the expectations of the others in the group for their sake?

Self-Deception

When we look in the mirror to examine ourselves, there is a natural human tendency to see only our goodness, strengths, positive features, and virtuous personality traits. There is an innate resistance to perceiving our dark side, weaknesses, negative qualities, and deficiencies. This tendency results in an inflated, incomplete, and inaccurate perception of ourselves. We mistakenly believe we possess genuine self-awareness, when in reality we do not. Our personal self-deception often keeps us in the dark about our true selves. Self-deception also results in ethical blindness—an inability to perceive ourselves and our conduct as being unethical.

My son David taught me a lesson about my own self-deception and blindness. When David was a sophomore in high school, he played football and was a starter on the varsity squad. I was a proud parent as I sat in the stands and watched him perform. After David's first game, I noticed that his pass-blocking skills could use improvement. The following day, I spoke to him about this and told him I could help with this skill. I took him out in the yard and told him to rush at me like a defensive lineman. I told him I would demonstrate the proper pass-blocking skills he needed to develop.

He naturally resisted my efforts, smiling and laughing as I urged him to let me show him a few techniques. He told me he could easily hurt me if I persisted. He told me I was an old man, out of shape, and even if I did know something about pass blocking, I learned it a long time ago when football was played under different rules. I did not have these same perceptions, so I would not let him off the hook.

Finally, David resigned himself to the fact that he had to endure this lesson from his father. He positioned and readied himself. I got down in a three-point stance. I called a snap count and rose up to block him. I was intent on protecting my imaginary quarterback.

I don't remember much after the snap count. I felt a sharp initial pain in my chest and my chin. I recall being sent backward in the air, landing on my tailbone, feeling excruciating pain shooting up through my spine. I recall my back hitting the ground and hearing the breath rush out of my lungs. I lost consciousness when my head whiplashed back onto the ground. All of this occurred in less than two seconds!

When I awoke, David was standing over me, peering into my eyes and laughing so hard that tears ran down his face. He muttered something about how silly I looked, twitching on the ground and gasping for breath. He helped me up, and I never again offered to help him with his pass-blocking techniques or any other aspect of football.

This was a good lesson for me in self-deception. You see, David weighed 210 pounds, was as strong as an ox, and was physically fit. I, on the other hand, was 42 years old, a bit out of shape, somewhat overweight, and getting gray. But for some unknown reason, when I looked in the mirror before going out with David and making a fool of myself, I saw and believed myself to be a physically fit, strong, 18-year-old mass of steel and sex appeal!

This is how insidious self-deception in ethics can be. You can lose total perspective of yourself and never know that you are suffering from ethical blindness.

Greed

The relentless pursuit of money, power, and fame is a major reason why many people engage in unethical conduct. There isn't much I can say to expound on this topic, other than saying that if left unchecked and unbalanced by notions of goodness and virtue, greed, in one of its many forms, will cause unethical conduct.

Conditioned Unthinking Reflexes

As outlined in previous chapters, each of us is subject and vulnerable to a variety of emotional responses, internalizations, and conditioned reflexes. These unthinking, almost automatic human responses cause much of the unethical conduct we see today. People simply do not pause to think and carefully consider their options before deciding on a course of conduct. Instead, they too often encounter a dilemma, react emotionally, and behave without exercising reflective judgment.

A Few Personal Questions

I'm sure there are many other reasons why people engage in unethical conduct. My list is not a thorough and exhaustive compilation. It represents a starting point to consider in your examination of why you have acted unethically in your life.

I encourage you to examine your own life and reflect a moment on those instances in which you might have been unethical. You should pause, consider, and identify why you took a particular unethical path or made a decision that you or others believed to be unethical. It is in such contemplation that insight, growth, and learning can occur.

Can you identify the causes of your past unethical conduct? What reasons have you used to justify your past misconduct?

*Authenticity
begins with knowing
your ethical type and
your ethical preferences.*

10

What Are Ethical Types?

There are seven ways in which people have incorporated ethical principles into their actual decision making. These approaches represent seven ethical typologies or preferences to personal decision making during an ethical or moral crisis. I refer to these as *ethical types*. Do you know your personal ethical preferences? Do you know your ethical type?

The seven preferences or ethical types are Egoism, Utilitarianism, Existentialism, Divine Command, Deontology, Conformism, and Eclectic.

Egoism

Egoism's central and fundamental principle is that when you are confronted by an ethical dilemma, the right thing to do is to choose or undertake the action that is in your best self-interest. Egoism is that inner drive that compels you to seek, maximize, and promote the greatest good for yourself. It is a results-oriented preference that causes you to analyze the possible consequences under a variety of options, and then select the alternative that will be best *for you.*

You adopt Egoism as your primary ethical type if you consistently focus on yourself, without regard for the consequences others might experience; your spiritual principles; the duties and obligations you owe to others; and how others feel about your decision.

Although Egoism has a negative emotional aura for many individuals, it is the underlying basis of the free-market enterprise system. Egoism was promoted by Adam Smith, the most popular of the free-market enterprise believers. Smith wrote that if each person in a society pursued his or her own self-interests, this focus on self would result in the fairest and most efficient distribution of goods, services, and wealth.

People who are highly influenced by Egoism tend to be survivors who are analytical and acutely aware of the consequences and implications of their conduct. Because the ethical choices of those who embrace Egoism do not take into account the needs of others, their choices result in harsh consequences for the rest of the world. This can make family, business, and social relationships difficult to maintain.

Egoism is found in much of our society. We see it a lot in business, entertainment, and sports, where highly paid executives, entertainers, and athletes sell themselves to the highest bidder in order to achieve financial independence. The outrageous antics and personal behaviors of Dennis Rodman and Madonna are good examples of egoism. The financial benefits each has derived justify, in their minds, the extreme and questionable conduct that has made them famous.

There are certainly times when Egoism is justified—when your life is threatened, or when others will not be harmed by your conduct. There are other occasions when it certainly raises cause for concern.

To what extent do you prefer and demonstrate Egoism in your ethical decisions? What decision or course of conduct have you recently undertaken that was purely in your self-interest? How often do you do this?

Utilitarianism

Utilitarianism is associated with the historical writings of Jeremy Bentham and John Stuart Mill. Its central and fundamental principle is that one should, when resolving ethical dilemmas, choose the path that is in the collective best interests of the greatest number of people. Utilitarianism requires you to seek the greatest good for the greatest number of people.

Like Egoism, Utilitarianism is a results-oriented prefer-ence. If you are influenced by this moral preference, you look at the consequences of your action in relation to how it will affect others. Unlike Egoism's focus on self, Utilitarianism focuses on the welfare of others. This is done without regard for the eventual consequences to self, spiritual principles, your sense of duty, or how others might feel about the decision you make.

The Utilitarian preference does not easily accommodate minority views and interests. It often results in consequences that are harsh and sometimes harmful to those whose needs and interests do not coincide with the greater good. The impact of a Utilitarian decision falls disproportionately upon a small group of individuals whose needs will be sacrificed so that the larger population will benefit.

To what extent do you use Utilitarianism in your moral decision making? How often do you sacrifice your self-interests or the interests of the minority in order to advance the needs and interests of others?

Existentialism

Existentialism was made popular by the writings of Søren Kierkegaard, Jean-Paul Sartre, and Albert Camus. Existential-ism's central principle is that when confronted with an ethical dilemma, you should look within yourself for the right moral path to follow, and that you should make a conscious choice to follow your deeper, inner sense of what is right and wrong. If you feel a strong drive to act in accordance with what you believe to be the inner purity of your heart or you feel com-pelled "to be true to yourself," then you are heavily influenced by Existentialism.

Existentialism is an ethical preference that is evidenced by a need and desire to focus on how you feel and the nature of your inner state of being. This preference is grounded on human autonomy and the conscious exercise of free will. Although a person who is heavily influenced by Existentialism might consider external consequences, spiritual principles, duties, or the influence of others in the deliberation of what is right or wrong, the ultimate deciding factor will be the person's inner, intuitive feeling of right and wrong.

One of the challenges of Existentialism is that human internalizations—such as personal biases, prejudices, emotions, thoughts, denials, and deceptions—make it very difficult to discover and express the authentic inner purity of the human heart.

To what extent are you influenced by Existentialism? Does your personal conduct reflect your inner purity?

Divine Command

Divine Command or Divine Inspiration (as it is sometimes referred to), is an ethical preference evident in the belief that when confronted by an ethical dilemma, you should follow the word of God, as reflected in scripture, religious doctrines, or spiritual teachings. It is based on the principle that God's will must be obeyed, and that you should subordinate human desires and temptations to God's laws.

Divine Command is not limited to a particular religious sect or denomination. It encompasses all religious beliefs: Christian, Jewish, Islamic, Buddhist, Hindu, Taoist, etc. Regardless of your individual religious affiliation, if you look to God's word to resolve ethical dilemmas, then you are heavily influenced by Divine Command.

The Divine Command preference provides clear and straightforward answers to ethical dilemmas for those who are influenced by it. Such individuals tend to accept God's word and act accordingly, and they expect others to do the same.

There is great diversity of belief across the religious spectrum. This sometimes makes it difficult to discover, interpret, and consistently follow God's word. At times, God's word is misinterpreted by man and is used as an instrument of evil by misguided and disturbed individuals.

Is Divine Command an important and relevant influence in your ethical decision making?

Deontology

Deontology's central and fundamental principle is that ethical dilemmas are best resolved by following certain prescribed duties or obligations that exist or are imposed by virtue of a person's existence as a human being, in affiliation with a cultural, societal, professional, business, or other group or occupation. Deontology is a preference grounded on the belief that ethical dilemmas are best resolved by following the established rules, codes of conduct, and duties prescribed by a recognized authority. When confronted with an ethical dilemma, a person influenced by Deontology will search for an applicable or governing duty or obligation; once it's identified, he or she will act in accordance with it. Consequently, external consequences to self or others, personal feelings, spiritual principles, and the influence of others are not relevant factors in determining the right thing to do.

Most cultures, societies, professions, organizations, industry groups, and businesses have developed elaborate codes of conduct that their members are expected to follow. These prescriptions offer clear-cut answers and outline sanctions for violations. Some philosophical writers have developed specific duties that they advocate as core human duties and responsibilities owed to other humans. These duties typically include the following: Keep promises. Do no harm to others. Help others. Act reasonably and prudently in relation to others. Pay for your mistakes. Take care of your family. Do not lie, cheat, or steal.

The key to understanding Deontology is to remember that you are obligated to see your duty and to do it. To what extent are you influenced by Deontology? What duties and responsibilities do you believe you owe to others?

Conformism

Conformism's central and fundamental principle is that when confronted with an ethical dilemma, a person ought to look to family, friends, colleagues, or a relevant social peer group and undertake an action or resolve the dilemma in a manner consistent with the perceived values and expectations of that group.

A person who is influenced by Conformism will avoid decisions and actions that conflict with the expectations of the relevant peer group. Peer pressure (the inherent human need to be accepted as a member of a group), concern for what others will think, and the need to avoid criticism and ridicule are concerns for a person who follows Conformism. Adolescents are particularly vulnerable to this preference.

Conformism keeps you close to societal mores if your relevant peer group is sufficiently broad and representative of society at large. However, Conformism interferes with individual reflective judgment. It can result in adverse consequences when the relevant peer group's influence is too strong or misaligned with society at large. Gang activity, mob behavior, religious group suicide cults, and hate groups are extreme examples of what can happen with this ethical type. To what extent do you consider the expectations of your peer group before you act? Are you a Conformist ethical type?

The Eclectic Type

The Eclectic ethical preference is one that blends and relies on two or more of the previously described ethical types. It results from the competing influences of the various ethical preferences you might experience. When confronted with an ethical dilemma, someone who is influenced by the Eclectic preference will take into account the influence of each preference, and will refrain from relying solely on one of them as the guiding basis of behavior.

You are probably strongly influenced by the Eclectic preference if you prefer to gather information and deliberate about an ethical decision by looking at the following: how your decision will affect you; how it will affect others; how you will feel about it and whether or not your decision will reflect your genuine self; how God's word might guide your decision, whether or not you have certain duties you must fulfill; and how others will view your decision.

The competing influences for a person who is an Eclectic often cause ethical decision making to be an agonizing and difficult process. A person who is influenced by the Eclectic preference will on occasion appear to act inconsistently with prior decisions and conduct.

To what extent do you rely on several ethical preferences in resolving your ethical dilemmas? Are you an Eclectic?

Discovering Your Ethical Type

Egoism, Utilitarianism, Existentialism, Divine Command, Deontology, Conformism, and Eclectic represent seven different ways of resolving moral dilemmas. Each person has a preferred way of resolving ethical dilemmas. This primary preference is referred to as an *ethical type.* You are influenced, to some extent, by each of the ethical types, but if you honestly examine your past conduct, you should be able to determine which of the seven ethical preferences has most influenced your personal conduct. You will also be able to determine the extent to which you are influenced by secondary ethical types.

Take a moment now and do this. Recall a time when you faced a difficult ethical decision. What did you do? What ethical preference was the basis of your conduct at that time?

Did you focus on what was best for you? Were you concerned with what might be best for others? Did you go within to find your inner purity and act in a way that was reflective of this inner state of being? Did you look to God for inspiration? Did you fulfill your duties and obligations? Did you conform your conduct to the expectations of others? Did you seek to incorporate the ethical prescriptions of several different types?

Can you now identify your **primary** ethical type? Can you identify the extent to which you are influenced by the other **secondary** ethical types?

Additional Self-Discovery

Knowing your ethical type or ethical preference is a good starting point for additional self-discovery. Ask yourself the following questions:

- Is your stated ethical type truly reflective of the way you resolve ethical dilemmas?

- Should you continue to rely on this ethical preference?

- Can you articulate why you prefer this ethical type?

- Do any of the other ethical types have merit or value?

- Do any of the other ethical types appeal to you?

- Are there situations in which one of the other ethical types might be more appropriate?

- Can you rank how the secondary ethical types influence your personal conduct?

Understanding Others

Once you have achieved an understanding of your own ethical type, you can use the ethical typology to gain an understanding and appreciation of how others resolve, justify, and defend their ethical positions.

If you develop an appreciation of each ethical type and listen carefully to what is being said during an ethical discussion, you will soon be able to recognize the underlying ethical types that other people rely on. This insight will give you a deeper understanding of the ethical constitutions of others and why they hold certain beliefs. This awareness will also help you understand that human belief systems are as diverse as race, gender, age, and religion. Hopefully, this knowledge will help you develop a greater tolerance of opposing views.

You can begin to enhance your understanding of others by doing the following:

- Tell others about the seven ethical types.

- Share with them your primary ethical type and secondary preferences.

- Ask your spouse, children, family, friends, and colleagues to characterize how they perceive your ethical type.

- Listen carefully to others as they speak. Observe their behavior for clues as to their ethical preferences.

- Make inquiries and ask questions of others to identify and explain the ethical or moral basis for their choices and personal conduct.

A Tool of Communication

Knowing the seven ethical types can also help you communicate, persuade, and influence others in a powerful and effective way. If you are engaged in a discussion in which you are attempting to persuade a colleague to adopt a particular view on an issue, your chances of success are increased and enhanced if you know your colleague's ethical type.

Have you ever attempted to persuade another person to adopt your ethical perspective on an issue by bombarding them with facts, figures, analysis, and arguments that are grounded on your own ethical beliefs and preferences? Didn't you become frustrated when your arguments failed to persuade this person to accept your ethical position?

Your failure should not be surprising. It should be understandable when you realize that not everyone shares your ethical type and preference. You should recognize that if the other person's ethical type is different from yours, this person will most likely reach a substantially different conclusion than yours.

It is important to keep in mind that Utilitarianism is incompatible with Egoism, and Existentialism is substantially different from Deontology, Conformism, and Divine Command. Therefore, two people of differing preferences arguing about an ethical dilemma is essentially like trying to force the proverbial round peg into a square hole. To be successful in such an argument, you must know the other person's ethical type and present ethical arguments based on his or her ethical preferences, not yours. In other words, you must shape the peg to fit into the other person's square. You do this by knowing what each ethical type requires and knowing the person's ethical type, and then creating arguments consistent with that person's ethical type to support your ethical conclusion. If you do this, you will find greater success in communicating and influencing others.

*Knowing your
core values can help you
live a more virtuous life.*

A core value represents that which you believe in and hold to be of utmost importance in your life.

11

What Is a Core Ethical Value?

I recently read a short biography of Benjamin Franklin. I learned that Franklin was born in 1706, the tenth son and fifteenth child of a Boston soap and candle maker. When he was 12 years old, Ben became an indentured apprentice to his brother, a printer. He spent five years learning the printing business, and when he was 17, he left Boston and journeyed to New York. He found no work there, so he resumed a long and arduous journey that took him to Philadelphia.

He arrived in Philadelphia with two shillings, a few pieces of tattered clothing, and four rolls of bread. He spent five years in youthful indulgence, but gradually emerged from this experience with a remarkable entrepreneurial talent. He ultimately established his own printing business and later took over the bankrupt *Pennsylvania Gazette* and published *Poor Richard's Almanac*.

Franklin served as clerk to the Pennsylvania Assembly until his own election as a representative. He also served as postmaster of Philadelphia. When Franklin was 42, he left business and embarked on a series of remarkable public ventures. His public accomplishments included establishing the first public subscription library; organizing Pennsylvania's first militia; and helping to create Philadelphia's first city watch, fire company, college, hospital, and fire insurance company. He served as grand master of Pennsylvania's Freemasons and founded the American Philosophical Society.

He took an active part in encouraging the paving and lighting of Philadelphia's streets.

Franklin also pioneered the development of what is now known as a "networking" group by establishing a club devoted to mutual improvement. The club required each member to profess a love for mankind and truth. Additionally, it required each member to take turns writing and presenting views on points of morality, politics, or natural philosophy. The group was devoted to mixing the business of doing good with the business of getting ahead. It did this by cultivating and utilizing professional and business connections.

The most impressive aspect of Franklin's life, in my view, was his personal project to "arrive at moral perfection." Remarkably, at age 25, Franklin developed a list of 13 virtues that he felt were desirable or necessary in order to achieve moral perfection. Franklin's virtues were temperance, silence, order, resolution, frugality, industry, sincerity, justice, moderation, cleanliness, tranquility, chastity, and humility.

Franklin's list of virtues, though impressive, is not as significant as his disciplined approach to learning and reflecting the values in his life.

He created a book in which he charted his daily progress toward moral perfection. His system was simple: He created fifty-two written pages in a journal, one page for each week of the year. He divided each page into seven columns, one for each day of the week. These columns were crossed by 13 lines, one for each of Franklin's virtues. At the end of each day, Franklin would reflect back and mark a little black spot for every fault he committed with respect to each virtue. In this way, Franklin maintained a written moral ledger of his progress.

Much is being written today about virtues and values and the need to incorporate ethical values into our business and professional lives. This resurgence is nothing but a reincarnation of Franklin's 13 virtues. Stephen Covey and other experts tout the importance of knowing and behaving in accordance with certain core ethical values or virtues. To my knowledge, none of these "values" or "virtues" experts have undertaken the discipline and effort reflected in Franklin's moral ledger.

Core ethical values are important in making ethical decisions and living a virtuous life. *Core ethical values* are those deeply held beliefs that you hold near and dear to your heart. They are concepts and principles that you treasure, value, and firmly embrace. Core ethical values are like beacons in the night that guide you along your desired moral path during turbulent times and in periods of moral ambiguity and ethical confusion.

Core ethical values include such concepts as loyalty, truth, honesty, respect, trust, friendship, family, fairness, equality, autonomy, freedom, courage, bravery, humility, health, kindness, happiness, and education. The list is endless. It is limited only by your imagination and by your choices of what is important. Do you know your core ethical values or virtues? Have you embarked on a personal journey to moral perfection? Have you developed your personal list of desirable virtues? What virtues are on the list? More importantly, is your conduct or behavior consistent with those virtues? Do you walk your own talk? What would your moral ledger reflect?

Core Values
The answers to the following questions will help you identify your core ethical values and the virtues that are important to you:

- Where and how do you spend your time?
- On what do you spend your money?
- What is truly important to you?
- How have you reacted to critical incidents or crises in your life?
- How have you treated other people during such times of crisis?
- What will others say about your core ethical values?

Ask others if your behavior reflects the values on your personal list. Be open to the process. Include your family, employees, friends, and customers in the inquiry. If you have the discipline, chart your progress in your own moral ledger.

From an organizational standpoint, develop a list of ethical values to guide the business behavior of your employees. Tell them your business philosophy and ethical expectations. Remind them frequently of these values. More importantly, demonstrate and reflect these values in your own conduct. Your employees might not listen to what you say, but they will critically examine your behavior and conduct.

Benjamin Franklin is known to have said this: "The way to wealth is as plain as the way to market. It depends chiefly on two words: industry and frugality. He who gets all he can honestly and saves all he gets will certainly become rich."

Franklin's successful private entrepreneurship and his public accomplishments clearly demonstrate that he walked his own talk. Will others say as much about you?

*Ethical virtuosity
is the capacity
to consistently identify,
confront, and resolve ethical
dilemmas in a manner
that reflects goodness.*

*Your personal intention
in a moment of ethical uncertainty
is a factor you ought to consider
before you act.*

Part II
The Seven Steps

*Doing
the right thing
requires a lot
from a person.*

12

Ethical Virtuosity

Ethical virtuosity refers to a person's ability to consistently identify, confront, and resolve ethical dilemmas in a manner that reflects goodness. It is demonstrated by personal conduct that is noble, honorable, and virtuous in all respects. In other words, it is consistently doing the right thing, at the right time.

How do you achieve ethical virtuosity? What must you do to be able to consistently do the right thing at the right time? I believe there are seven basic steps you need to take if you want to achieve ethical virtuosity.

First, you must look inward and discover a few things about yourself. Critically examine who you are, what you believe in, and what is truly important to you.

Second, you must search for, study, and evaluate the body of ethical knowledge that has been left to us by the great philosophers. This requires special effort, since the moral legacy of the great philosophers is a bit challenging to comprehend and apply in today's fast-paced, rapidly changing world of technology.

Third, you must develop a relevant, comprehensive, and meaningful ethical belief system. This requires that you identify, determine, choose, and develop your life's mission, personal beliefs, and core ethical values.

Fourth, you must learn and practice emotional discipline. This requires you to master your internalizations and other factors that get in the way of your achieving ethical virtuosity.

Fifth, you must consciously exercise, on a moment-by-moment basis, your individual human autonomy (your free will) to conform and align your behavior to your ethical belief system.

Sixth, you must demonstrate moral courage and personal accountability on a daily basis. To do this, you must know what each of these principles requires of you as a human being.

Seventh, you must develop an individual action plan that contains specific behavioral goals, personal commitments, and an evaluation system to track your progress.

If you undertake, complete, and practice the seven steps just outlined, you can achieve ethical virtuosity and come close to the moral perfection that Benjamin Franklin and others have sought throughout history.

Being
an authentic person
requires that you take
an inward journey.

*Spend time in
contemplation with yourself.*

13

Step 1: Develop Self-Awareness

Socrates is believed to have said, "Know thyself." He also said, "The unexamined life is not worth living."

Both of these ancient platitudes, concise in form and simple in statement, reveal the first step toward achieving ethical virtuosity—engaging in a process of self-assessment that leads to self-knowledge.

This first step involves critical self-examination, personal insight, and genuine self-awareness. It requires getting in touch with your true inner core.

People who know themselves are able to articulate what is truly important in their lives. They have a strong sense of purpose in life. They know their core ethical values. They can easily relate and defend the ethical principles that guide their lives. They know their ethical type. They are able to define what ethics, integrity, and good moral character mean in their lives. They know their personal failings and are able to identify those occasions when their behavior conflicts with their ethical values. They know why they have acted unethically in the past. They know the extent to which their ethical beliefs are shaped and influenced by parents, friends, media, past experience, education, culture, internalizations, conditioned reflexes, and reflective judgment. They know their preferred defense mechanisms and how these rationalizations, projections, and denials interfere with their ethical decision making. They have a genuine knowledge of their authentic self.

Do you know as much about yourself? Can you relate the same information concerning *your* ethical constitution? More importantly, will you take the time to do the work that will allow you to genuinely know the essence of your ethical core? If you have reflected on and answered the questions I have presented throughout this work, you will find yourself remarkably insightful concerning your ethical state of being. If you have not done this work, I can only urge you to revisit these questions and complete these important exercises.

Becoming self-aware involves much more than the ethical inquiries I have presented thus far. The process of self-discovery goes beyond your ethical personality. Here are some of the other areas of inquiry you ought to undertake as a means of connecting with yourself.

Do you have a strong sense of your purpose and meaning in this life? What is that purpose? Have you captured the purpose in a written statement of your life's mission? Will you do so now?

What is the general condition of your life? Are you genuinely happy? Do you feel passion and excitement in your personal relationships and in your professional work? What is the source of the joy you experience in your life? What sadness and disappointments are you experiencing? What is the true source of this sorrow?

Is your life balanced? Do you spend quality time fulfilling your family obligations, spiritual yearnings, physical and health needs, professional obligations, and community responsibilities? Are you neglecting one or more of these fundamental dimensions in your life?

What motivates you? What are the things you would like to do in your life that you have not yet been able to do? What is really keeping you from doing these things?

What are your hopes and dreams? Do you have a vision of an uplifting and positive future? Are you actively working to bring about your hopes, dreams, and visions, or have you given up? What obstacles and challenges are preventing you from realizing your future? Are you willing to make the personal sacrifices to create your future? Are you willing to change?

Who are you? What are your strengths? What are your weaknesses? Are you working to overcome your weaknesses? What are your unique gifts and talents? Are you using these talents in a constructive manner? What are your vulnerabilities? What are your bad habits that you need to change? Do you know how you sabotage or get in the way of your own success?

What do you stand for? How do you define yourself? What is truly important to you? What do you believe in? What do you feel most strongly about in your life? What do you cherish and value?

What do others say about you? How do they perceive you? How will you be remembered? What legacies will you leave behind? Do you genuinely walk your talk? Where have you not done so?

What mistakes have you made in your life? What have you learned from these events?

Are your personal relationships fulfilling and meaningful? Do you need to make changes? How can you improve and enhance your relationships?

What are you missing in your life? What voids do you experience? What are you willing to do about it?

These are just a few of the fundamental life questions you need to address as you strive toward ethical virtuosity. Spend quality time reflecting on these matters. Your answers will provide valuable and powerful insights.

Knowledge is power.

14

Step 2: Seek Ethical Knowledge

The second step toward ethical virtuosity involves searching for, studying, and acquiring ethical knowledge. The great moral philosophers have left us a vast and rich body of ethical writings and insights. For example, the ancient Greek philosophies of Socrates, Plato, Aristotle, Epictetus, and others are still relevant today. The teachings of Jesus, Martin Luther, Thomas Aquinas, Thomas Merton, St. Augustine, and others are relied upon by millions of Christians as a way of finding God and living a moral life. The teachings and sayings of Lao-tzu, Buddha, and Confucius are followed by millions in the Asian world. There is not a day that goes by without someone quoting Benjamin Franklin, Søren Kierkegaard, John Stuart Mill, Thomas Hobbes, and Jean-Paul Sartre, to name but a few.

If you want to achieve ethical virtuosity, you must cultivate an intellectual thirst for the insights of the great moral philosophers. You need to read and study the classical writings on ethics. You need to seek out and evaluate newly emerging ethical thought.

The ethical knowledge you gain as a result of your study of the moral legacy left by the great philosophers will add richness and depth to your life and help you do the right thing at the right time.

To induce you to begin your own ethical journey through our moral legacy, I have selected a few philosophers for you to consider. Short, highly condensed summaries of their major ethical thoughts are presented here. As is the case with any effort to summarize, the paragraphs that follow are not meant to be complete and exhaustive expositions of each philosopher's work. The summaries present only a few of the major themes of each philosopher. Hopefully, this limited treatment of certain secular philosophers will stimulate your own in-depth study and review.

The following summaries do not include the teachings of the great spiritual figures, prophets, and leaders, since such a task is far beyond the scope of this work on ethics. There are voluminous works on spiritual teachings available elsewhere.

Protagoras of Abdera

Protagoras (490–421 B.C.) was one of the first men to declare himself a "Sophist"—one who traveled throughout the Greek world, offering instruction in return for money. Consequently, he arduously believed that virtue could be taught. His writings reveal him to have been an *individualistic relativist.* He believed that reality and truth were individual matters that depended on a person's unique perspectives and view of the world. Thus, what was truth, reality, goodness, or right or wrong for one individual was not necessarily the truth, reality, goodness, or right or wrong for another.

Understandably, Protagoras conceived of law as a necessary agreement between members of a society to ensure human survival. Protagoras noted that law represents human customs that serve as restraints on individual will, guiding and defining the limits within which one can act.

Socrates

Socrates (469–399 B.C.) lived his life as a teacher. He is perhaps best remembered for his methodology of questioning and making constant inquiries into the essential nature of things and concepts. The Socratic method of teaching, characterized by the teacher's practice of posing a barrage of questions to his students, is one of the modern-day legacies of Socrates.

Socrates' overall philosophy included concepts such as the importance of the soul, the need to care for the soul, introspection, self-examination, happiness, wisdom, self-control, and self-mastery.

Socrates conceived of the soul as intelligence and character. He sought to improve the soul, and believed that virtue and excellence were the critical elements. He believed that piety, justice, courage, prudence, beauty, and health were virtues that one ought to develop and demonstrate in one's life.

Socrates taught that self-mastery and self-control are crucial if one desires to live a virtuous life. He recognized the adverse effects of human passion and impulses on the soul. He urged people to develop a strong inner life of contemplation and to reason, to bring to bear their intellect, and to practice discipline as a means of understanding oneself, acquiring wisdom, and overcoming human desires. Socrates taught that self-control allows freedom from human passions, and that the lack of self-mastery and self-control causes one to remain a slave to human impulses.

Socrates also believed that a person should not engage in conduct based on a personal belief of its goodness without also understanding the underlying basis for that belief.

He is believed to have said that if you want to know a man's morals, look at his personal conduct, for it is in such behavior that a man's morals are evident.

Socrates was charged with sedition and conspiracy. His critics feared him and believed that his teachings were corrupting the youth of the state. He defended himself in his trial, but was convicted and sentenced to death. His friends were prepared to help him escape and avoid the death penalty, but Socrates declined the offer of help. In a grand gesture of self-mastery and control, he complied with the authorities by consuming the deadly hemlock cocktail that brought about his death.

Plato

Plato (429–347 B.C.) was a student of Socrates and a prolific writer. He echoed Socrates' focus on the soul. He believed it is of great importance to educate the soul, understand it, and control it through the exercise of reason. He believed the soul to be capable of self-direction toward goodness.

Plato conceived of the soul as consisting of three parts: the rational, spirit, and desire. He believed that the rational component is capable of maintaining a balance between spirit and desire, but that this task can only be accomplished through the powerful exercise of the mind.

Aristotle

Aristotle (384–322 B.C.) studied in Athens under Plato. He was summoned to be the tutor of the young 13-year-old Alexander the Great. When Alexander assumed the throne, Aristotle returned to Athens and established his own school.

Aristotle believed that all human conduct is guided by its ends or goals. He taught that humans have freedom of choice over their conduct. Aristotle believed that the human soul is comprised of two parts: a rational part and a nonrational part. The rational part is the place of intellectual virtue, while the nonrational is the location of appetites and of desire.

He conceived of humans as having to constantly choose between virtue and vice. According to Aristotle, vice is the result of excessive or defective activity. Virtue, on the other hand, is the midpoint between excess and defect. For example, courage, a virtuous state of being, is the middle ground between rashness (excess) and cowardice (defect).

Aristotle believed that the health and happiness of the soul can be achieved through training and the development of good habits, and that a person can become virtuous as a result of constant adherence to a pattern of good living.

Aristotle promoted adherence to the following virtues: courage, temperance, magnificence, magnanimity, proper ambition, patience, truthfulness, wittiness, friendliness, modesty, and righteous indignation.

Epicurus

The philosophy and beliefs of Epicurus (341–270 B.C.) stand in contrast to those of Socrates, Plato, and Aristotle. Epicurus believed that goodness and virtue are found by pursuing pleasure and avoiding pain. Thus, personal sensation and physical pleasure were seen as the pathways to knowledge and virtue. This view did not imply that one can engage in activities to an extreme or excess, for to do so would inevitably result in pain. Epicurus taught that one should enjoy food and delight in the pleasure it provides, but if it is consumed in excess, the individual will experience discomfort and pain. Epicurus' ethics required a balance of pleasure and pain, accepting some pain for subsequent pleasure and rejecting pain that leads to greater discomfort.

Epicurus valued the following virtues: justice, temperance, and courage.

Epictetus

Epictetus (50–125 A.D.) was born a slave and was brought to Rome and educated. Released upon his master's death, he became a teacher and focused on sharing concepts of how to live a virtuous life. He believed that the virtuous life consists of knowledge, practice, truth, and freedom.

Epictetus was a Stoic philosopher. His views on freedom are particularly noteworthy. He observed that freedom is not the power to do as one desires, but rather that freedom is found in being able to understand one's limits—particularly what is and what is not within one's control. Epictetus believed that by accepting our limitations and training our desires to accept that truth, we can experience freedom. In yielding to the desire for control and for things that we cannot have, we lose personal freedom.

Epictetus taught that we cannot choose the external circumstances we encounter—only how we will respond to them and how we feel about them.

Like Socrates, Plato, and Aristotle, Epictetus believed in the power of the mind, rational thought, and the development of good habits as a means of living a virtuous life.

It is reported that Epictetus' teacher, during an educational session, began twisting Epictetus' leg. Epictetus sat stoically and said, "You are going to break my leg." When the teacher continued and the leg was broken, Epictetus calmly remarked, "I told you so." This example of self-control epitomizes Epictetus' philosophy of Stoicism.

Marcus Aurelius

Marcus Aurelius (121–180 A.D.) was the Emperor of Rome from 161–180 A.D. He, like Epictetus, was a Stoic philosopher. He believed that each person should accept his fate, destiny, and position in life, and fulfill his role to the best of his ability. He believed that ill will or mistreatment cannot hurt a person without that person's permission or against that person's will or desire.

According to Marcus Aurelius, freedom is gained by accepting and responding in a rational manner, rather than responding in a highly agitated and emotional manner. He reportedly said that the quality of one's life is dependent on the quality of one's thoughts, echoing the belief in the power of the human mind and the need for reason and rational thought.

Niccolò Machiavelli

Niccolò Machiavelli (1469–1527 A.D.) possessed a dark and evil view of the world. His observations of his society and culture led him to believe that people are corrupt, evil, and self-serving. He observed that people endlessly desire and lust for power, pleasure, and profit, and get caught up in an intense, ruthless, and competitive struggle for survival.

Machiavelli believed that to survive in such an environment, one has to seek, grab, hold, and exercise power for self-preservation. He did not believe in the Christian principle of self-sacrifice.

Machiavelli was most likely heavily influenced by the Egoism preference.

Friedrich Nietzsche

Friedrich Nietzsche (1844–1900 A.D.) believed that the natural desire of a person is to dominate others and to reshape the world to fit one's own preferences, views, and perspectives. He believed that people have unrestricted desires for conquest, passionate love, and mystical ecstasy, and that we are all engaged in a fierce struggle for power and dominance. Nietzsche observed that people will readily do what they can to gain power.

He was a critic of Christianity, believing that traditional Christian values of goodness, meekness, and servility created a culture that destroyed the drive for excellence, achievement, and self-realization. Nietzsche believed that equality, selflessness, meekness, humility, sympathy, and pity are qualities of weakness.

Nietzsche embraced and believed in individualistic values, such as the spirit of nobility, self-assertion, daring, creativity, passion, excellence, and the affirmation of life, struggle, and conquest.

Nietzsche's views identify and reveal him to be aligned with the Egoism preference.

Thomas Hobbes

Another philosopher heavily influenced by Egoism was Thomas Hobbes (1588–1679 A.D.), who felt that all human conduct arises out of an inherent need for self-preservation. He believed that the human drive for self-preservation causes a perpetual state of war in which everyone has a natural right to anything they need in order to survive. People will therefore do anything in their own judgment to get out of the state of war.

Hobbes counseled that the only way to get out of the chaos and war of survival is to have a strong government based on a social contract—a voluntary agreement in which everyone gives up certain rights in exchange for certain benefits and privileges.

Adam Smith

Adam Smith (1723–1790 A.D.) believed that humans are imbued by God with powerful instincts and passions that can result in behaviors that are ultimately beneficial to all. Specifically, Smith noted that humans possess an innate concern for their individual self-interest. He believed that competition among various self-interests is good and will result in the just and equitable distribution of goods and services, thereby benefiting society at large. Smith was a strong proponent of Egoism.

David Hume

The ethical thoughts of David Hume (1711–1776 A.D.) are centered around the premise that moral convictions are based on feelings, rather than on reason. Hume believed that morality or a sense of right and wrong arises only when people react to circumstances and develop feelings of approval or disapproval. Thus, Hume advocated an emotional or intuitive model of ethics that diminished the importance of rational thought.

Clearly, Hume would encourage us to make ethical choices based on our feelings rather than absolute rules of conduct or reason. This emphasis on feelings rather than logic and rational thought distinguishes Hume from most moral philosophers.

Jean Jacques Rousseau

Jean Jacques Rousseau (1712–1778 A.D.) believed that man is by nature inherently good, and that it is society that is the cause of all corruption and vice. He believed that each person, in his natural state, possesses a healthy self-love that is turned into venal pride when one seeks the approval or good opinion of others in society. This conformity with society causes people to lose touch with their true inner self, and results in a loss of freedom. Rousseau believed that the path to freedom is to remain true to yourself. His beliefs help form the basis for the Existentialism preference.

Søren Kierkegaard

Søren Kierkegaard (1813–1855 A.D.), born in Copenhagen, Denmark, is considered by many to be the father of Existentialism. Kierkegaard noted that in the process of daily living, the individual encounters ambiguous and uncertain life situations that force him to choose between two or more incompatible alternatives. In choosing a moral path, Kierkegaard rejected the existence of objective tests of morality, believing instead that moral standards can only be individually chosen. In the end, he said, the choice of the individual is all that matters. Kierkegaard encouraged individualistic reflection, contemplation, and freedom to choose one's own moral standards.

Jean-Paul Sartre

Jean-Paul Sartre (1905–1980 A.D.) noted that the moral direction of a person's life is always in question. Like Kierkegaard, he believed that we exist in situations and that these life circumstances undoubtedly affect us at a personal level. However, Sartre believed that the nature and quality of our existence in such situations is a matter of personal choice.

He believed that we possess individual freedom, which he defined as having the ability to choose what we will be and how we will see the world. Thus the type of person we will become is dependent on our individual consciousness and how we choose to live our life. This freedom makes us solely responsible for ourselves.

Sartre proclaimed that we as individuals are defined by our choices and our actions. His emphasis on individual freedom and choice aligns him with the Existentialism school of thought.

Jeremy Bentham

Jeremy Bentham (1748–1832 A.D.) believed that humans are motivated by the desire to experience pleasure and avoid pain. This, you should recognize, is the same philosophical view as Epicurus. Bentham, however, took this moral outlook one step further by proclaiming that the rightness or wrongness of an action can be judged by its tendency toward consequences that are pleasurable or painful.

Bentham believed that pleasure is the only good, and that one should undertake action that generates the greatest pleasure. When this principle is coupled with Bentham's view that our duty is to promote pleasure for everyone equally, the result is a form of Utilitarianism known as *Hedonistic Utilitarianism.*

John Stuart Mill

John Stuart Mill (1806–1873 A.D.) was also a Utilitarian philosopher who believed that an action is right if it brings about a greater balance of good over bad consequences. Good was defined by Mill as social welfare, rather than pure pleasure (as Bentham believed). Mill pragmatically recognized that people always act to maximize their own pleasure, but he advocated that general social welfare ought to be one of the pleasures they seek.

Immanuel Kant

Immanuel Kant (1724–1804 A.D.) was a Deontological philosopher who believed that there are certain universal, absolute principles of right and wrong that transcend time and culture. Kant believed that these universal truths or duties can be discovered through reason, and that by following these moral absolutes, a person can achieve a virtuous life.

Kant formulated one such universal duty, which he referred to as the Categorical Imperative. This principle was embodied in two formulations. The first formulation states that you ought to act the way you want others to act in a similar situation. It is a version of the old rule, "Do unto others as you would have them do unto you." The second formulation states that you should treat others with human dignity and never use people as a means to an end.

Kant's Categorical Imperative represents an absolute rule of moral behavior, and puts him within the Deontological tradition.

William Goodwin

William Goodwin (1756–1836 A.D.) was another philosopher who followed the Deontological tradition. He believed that reason leads to truth and truth leads to justice. He held that education and environment determine one's character, but that all humans have the potential to be rational and virtuous.

Goodwin proclaimed that humans have no inherent rights—only a fundamental moral duty to reveal benevolence. Although he was a proponent of reason, he did not exclude the need for affection during a moral deliberation of right and wrong. He recognized, however, that one's feelings have to be regulated during the deliberative process of seeking benevolence and human improvement.

Your Favorite Philosopher

Did the foregoing summaries leave you with any impressions? Did you develop an interest, liking, or preference for any particular philosopher's beliefs? Did any of the philosophers' concepts strike you as particularly meaningful? Did you develop a dislike or a negative reaction to any of them?

*You must have
a defined ethical
belief system
in order to be
an ethical person.*

*Can you identify, articulate,
and defend your ethical
belief system?*

15

Step 3: Develop an Ethical Belief System

The third step toward achieving ethical virtuosity requires that you develop your own unique ethical belief system. The components of your ethical belief system should include a personal mission statement; a compilation of your core ethical principles; a statement of your core ethical values; statements concerning how you view ethics, integrity, and character; a statement of your ethical mythologies; and a statement of the factors that influence your ethical beliefs.

If you have been diligent in answering the questions that were posed in the previous chapters of this work, you should be in a position to easily review your prior efforts, make a few revisions, and complete your ethical belief system.

If you have not yet done the work, now is the time. Resist your desire to read ahead. Overcome your natural hesitancy to put off answering the following questions:

- What does ethics require you to do?

- What are your ethical beliefs?

- What gets in the way of your achievement of ethics, integrity, and good moral character?

- What are your core values?

- How will others remember you?

- What is your purpose in life?

- What does ethics require of you?
- What does integrity mean to you?
- What are the essential aspects of your character?
- What gets in the way of your mastery of ethical virtuosity?

*What are the principles
that guide you in times
of moral ambiguity?*

You must know,
master, and control
your emotions.

16

Step 4: Practice Emotional Discipline

The fourth step toward ethical virtuosity involves mastering and controlling your emotions, impulses, internalizations, drives, and weaknesses. In its most simplistic expression, Step 4 is *practicing self-restraint.*

This dimension is important because your emotions, impulses, internalizations, drives, and weaknesses can be destructive forces that impair your ability to act in an ethical manner.

Emotion has the potential to interfere with your human capacity to reason. It can hinder and obscure your ability to accurately perceive and interpret reality. It can cause ethical blindness—the inability to perceive the existence of an ethical dilemma or the unethical aspects of your own conduct. It is important to be able to identify, manage, control, and understand the range of human emotions that occur during an ethical crisis, as well as to understand how these emotions can negatively affect your capacity to reason. Do not ignore these important skills.

Daniel Goleman reminds us in his best-selling work *Emotional Intelligence* that there is a neurological reason why humans tend to react emotionally (experience an internalization) before responding in a rational and logical manner.

According to Goleman, as we experience a life event, information about that occurrence is channeled through our senses and directed to the thalamus, a portion of our brain that processes and evaluates information before sending it to other parts of our brain for response. The two primary recipients of this neurological data are the amygdala and the neocortex.

The *amygdala* is the originator of our emotional reactions, our passions, and our initial impulses. It is also the location of our emotional memories. If our amygdala is lost or destroyed, we lose our capacity for feelings and all sense of personal meaning.

When information from the thalamus is received by the amygdala, a wide range of emotional reactions becomes possible. The amygdala evaluates the information within the context of the current event and past experiences. It then activates, initiates, or causes a particular emotional response.

The neurological pathway from the thalamus to the amygdala is extremely short and direct. From a biological, evolutionary standpoint, this direct and quick pathway was crucial to the survival of our species, since it allowed for speedy determination of whether to fight or flee a dangerous situation.

The *neocortex* is that part of our brain that activates and controls rational and logical thought. Like the amygdala, it receives information from the thalamus and initiates a response to the neurological data it receives. The neocortex's response, however, is not an emotional response. It is a response grounded in reason and reflective judgment. Another significant difference between the amygdala and the neocortex is that the neurological pathway to the neocortex is long and circuitous. Thus the neocortex receives its information from the thalamus much later than the amygdala, whose short and direct neurological pathway allows it to respond well before the neocortex.

The neocortex sends a signal to the amygdala in an effort to bring reasoning to the amygdala's response. However, the short, direct signal from the thalamus triggers a reaction from the amygdala prior to the filtered signal that arrives from the neocortex. The result is that impulsive feelings, triggered by the amygdala, tend to override the slower-arriving rational thoughts from the neocortex.

The amygdala's initial impulses can be managed by another part of the brain known as the *prefrontal lobes,* located at the end of the neocortex's long, circuitous neurological pathway. Thus the moderating affect of the prefrontal lobes kicks in after the initial impulsive reaction of the amygdala. This is the natural, biological reason why humans tend to react emotionally to life occurrences before or even without pausing, thinking, and reflecting upon an effective course of action.

People who possess ethical virtuosity have learned how to exercise emotional discipline, control their emotional responses, delay gratification, resist the impulses initiated by the amygdala, and bring to bear the full potential of their higher-level capacity to reason in such a way that ethical and responsible conduct occurs during an ethical crisis. In essence, people who possess ethical virtuosity have mastered themselves and their emotions.

Does your repertoire of personal skills include the ability to exercise emotional discipline? Are you a master of your own emotions? Can you delay personal gratification and resist your emotional impulses?

Here are a few strategies to help you master this dimension of ethical virtuosity. First, recognize and appreciate the underlying neurological dynamics that are at work. When you seek to control your emotions, drives, internalizations, impulses, and weaknesses, you are up against a formidable neurological opponent that has already triggered chemical reactions in your body. Heart rate, respiration, blood pressure, and perspiration are all elevated, most likely causing you to experience a heightened state of arousal or anxiety. You must be able to recognize the initial onset of these symptoms.

Second, you must resist the urge to take immediate responsive action. Remember, you need to give your neocortex time to receive the information and process it. Take a walk, disengage, count to ten—in other words, buy yourself some time. Distance yourself from the immediate circumstances so that you are not forced to respond until you are emotionally and intellectually ready to do so.

Third, allow the emotional wave, internalization, impulse, or drive to dissipate or vent in a healthy manner. Exercise works great for me. Expressing your feelings in a safe place, away from the circumstances, also works wonders. Find some strategy that works for you. The goal is to purge yourself as much as possible of the neurological responses that have been triggered.

Fourth, use the reflective judgment techniques outlined in the next chapter.

Fifth, find a stable, balanced, calm, and trusted friend or colleague to share with and discuss your situation and options. Avoid people who are easily excitable, biased, or highly emotional. They will only escalate what you already feel. What you need is a supportive outlet and a relaxed environment so that you can think clearly and make good decisions.

Remember: Your mind has tremendous power to affect how you will respond. Give it a chance to help you.

*Ethics requires
a conscious choice
to exercise your free will
to achieve a noble
and virtuous purpose.*

*You get to decide
what you will or will not
become.*

17

Step 5: Exercise Free Will

The fifth step toward achieving ethical virtuosity requires that you consciously exercise your free will toward a noble and virtuous end. The extent to which you can actually exercise your free will in such a manner depends on several factors.

First and foremost is your desire, motivation, and ultimate ability to follow the other six steps toward ethical virtuosity. Each step along the way is critical. If you genuinely know yourself, obtain ethical knowledge, develop an ethical belief system, practice emotional discipline, demonstrate moral courage and personal accountability, and implement an individual action plan, you have a much greater chance of exercising your free will in a virtuous manner when it most counts—when you are faced with the agonizing temptations and conflicting feelings and pressures of an ethical dilemma.

The second factor in exercising free will toward a noble and virtuous end is your ability to know, understand, and appreciate that you actually possess free will. Some people never realize this. If you can understand what free will really means, you have a good chance of achieving ethical virtuosity.

The third factor is your capacity to engage in reflective judgment, a disciplined process of critical thinking. Following such a process will help you master and control your free will.

Free Will

What is free will? What does this concept really mean? Can you define and explain it? Does it have personal significance in your life?

Free will is sometimes referred to as individual human autonomy. It refers to the notion that your heart, soul, mind, thoughts, feelings, and behavior are capable of individual direction toward goodness or evil. As a human being, you are endowed with personal freedom of choice. You have the ability to choose how you feel about and how you respond to life's many demands and challenges. You have the inherent human capacity to choose the type of person you will become, the direction your life will take, how you will see the world, and how you will think and feel about your life. In essence, free will gives you the ability to be the master of your own life.

Free will has been expressed in many different ways by the great philosophers. St. Augustine is reported to have said that the purity of the soul cannot be lost without our consent. Plato said that the human soul is capable of self-direction toward goodness. Epictetus observed that an individual cannot control his or her external circumstances, but can control and determine how he or she feels about and responds to them. Marcus Aurelius is noted to have said that personal happiness is dependent upon the quality of one's thoughts. All of these ancient concepts reflect a fundamental belief in the existence and the power of free will.

Recall the "Life's Paradigm" outlined in Chapter 5. This simple formulation has as its core and central foundation the principle of free will and human autonomy. Do you remember the paradigm? It says, in simplistic terms, that life presents challenges, demands, and dilemmas that trigger internalizations (thoughts, feelings, drives, impulses, etc.) that provide opportunities for us to choose how we will respond and define our character. When we make a choice, we exercise our free will.

Sometimes our choices are conscious, and at other times they are driven by our emotions, prejudices, biases, and unconscious thoughts. The real challenge with free will is to consistently make conscious choices toward goodness and to overcome the temptations, drives, and impulses that get in the way.

Do you genuinely recognize and truly honor your personal human autonomy or free will in your decisions and behavior, or are you a slave to your internalizations? Do you understand and appreciate the tremendous power and potential that free will affords you in your daily life and in shaping your own future?

Exercising your free will toward goodness is much easier said than done. This is why you need to learn and practice reflective judgment techniques. Following a disciplined process of reflection before you act gives you the opportunity to express your free will and free yourself from the bondage of your personal internalizations.

Reflective Judgment

Reflective judgment refers to a disciplined process of pausing, sorting out, thinking about, contemplating, and reflecting upon a situation before making a decision. It is a process of inner critical thinking and judgment that gives you the opportunity to control your internalizations and discover your authenticity by balancing your human emotions with your intellect and reason. The goal of reflective judgment is to help you consciously exercise your free will toward goodness and virtue.

Do you have a personal strategy or process that you rely on when you are confronted with an ethical dilemma, or do you rely instead on an undefined sense of intuition? To what extent do you actually engage in reflective judgment? What are the specific steps that you follow? What steps should you follow to assure your exercise of free will toward goodness and virtue?

A 12-Step Process

To help you create your own process of reflective judgment, I offer the following 12-step process for consideration. It is one of many avenues that can lead you to critical thinking and inner reflection. Examine it and develop your own disciplined process of reflective judgment.

1. Manage the initial emotional reaction.

Recognize that during an ethical crisis, you will experience a variety of emotional internalizations that will diminish your ability to consciously exercise your free will. Identify these emotional reactions and exercise emotional discipline as suggested in the previous chapter. Manage your emotional pathway so that you can bring to bear your intellectual capacities to reason. This means that you must reserve final judgment until the process of reflective judgment is complete.

2. Identify the real ethical issue.

Often, decisions and judgments are made without resolving the true underlying ethical issue or dilemma. Thus, it is important to identify, characterize, and articulate the specific ethical issue presented by the crisis.

3. Gather relevant facts.

Don't assume that you have all the pertinent facts necessary to render a wise and ethical decision. Devote time to confirming the existing facts. Ask yourself what other facts you should have in order to make an informed and ethical decision. Obtain them in an expeditious manner and consider how this information affects your decision.

4. Consider the law.

Determine if there are any applicable legal requirements or authorities that govern the decision. If so, then follow and adhere to the law, unless the law itself is manifestly immoral or unjust.

5. Ask others for input.

Don't hesitate to ask others for input or advice. It is helpful to obtain diverse opinions and perspectives. Weigh the advice carefully.

6. **Consider your ethical belief system.**

Remember that you have one primary ethical type or preference and that you are influenced by six other ethical preferences. Consider what these preferences require of you in this dilemma. Recall the guiding ethical principles that you have identified as being important to you. Determine what these principles mandate.

7. **Consider your core ethical values.**

Recall and consider your core ethical values. Remember that your core ethical values are the ideals and beliefs that you embrace and want reflected in all your decisions. Determine how your decision can incorporate and reflect your core ethical values.

8. **Make a decision.**

Remember that you have free will. You have the capacity to choose your path. Make a decision grounded on your ethical belief system and core ethical values. Make sure your decision is a conscious one that moves you closer to goodness. Bring to bear your intellect and powers of higher reasoning. Filter your emotions, but make sure that your decision is one that ultimately incorporates empathy, compassion, and human dignity.

9. **Let your decision ripen.**

Do not act immediately on your decision. Give yourself the opportunity to reconsider it in the light of a new day. Sleep on your decision before finalizing it.

10. **Ratify or change your decision.**

Once you have had the opportunity to reconsider your decision, you should either ratify it or change it based on your new thoughts and feelings. Don't hesitate to modify a prior decision if you have changed your thoughts about it.

11. Announce the decision.

If possible, tell others about your decision and your intended course of action. Going public has a powerful way of holding you accountable to the decision.

12. Act on the decision.

Implement your decision and behave in accordance with the principles that guided it.

This 12-step process is not complicated. It just requires discipline. If you follow these steps and bring integrity to the process, you will make more-enlightened decisions that reflect your free will and bring you closer to ethical virtuosity.

20 Questions

An alternative technique of reflective judgment is to develop a series of questions that you ask yourself when confronted with an ethical decision. Here are my questions. See if they can help you gain greater ethical insight.

1. Will my decision or conduct comply with the law?

2. Will my decision or conduct be consistent with my personal ethical belief system?

3. Will my decision or conduct reflect and promote my core ethical values?

4. What ethical principles or values ought to be the basis of my decision or conduct in this situation?

5. Have I considered the needs and interests of those who might be affected by my decision or conduct?

6. Will my decision or conduct be judged fair now and in the future?

7. Will I be proud of my decision or conduct?

8. What will my family think of me if they know or learn of my behavior?

9. Will my decision or conduct create value?

10. Will my decision or conduct move me closer to goodness and virtue?

11. Am I being pressured or unduly influenced by others?

12. Am I being driven by my emotions?

13. Have I filtered out my ego needs and my own self-interests?

14. Will my conduct reflect honesty, integrity, and truthfulness?

15. Are there spiritual concerns or principles I ought to consider?

16. What will be the consequences of my behavior?

17. Who will benefit from my decision?

18. Who will be harmed by my conduct?

19. Will my decision or conduct permit or encourage exploitation of others or greed?

20. Are there other alternatives I should consider?

My 20 questions represent a basic starting point for critical thinking, reflective judgment, and the conscious exercise of free will. What questions do *you* ask yourself when you are confronted with an ethical dilemma?

Moral courage
is the foundation that
makes ethical behavior possible.

18

Step 6: Demonstrate Moral Courage and Personal Accountability

The sixth step toward achieving ethical virtuosity is the most difficult to master. It requires you to cultivate and personally demonstrate attitudes of moral courage and personal accountability in your daily conduct and during times of moral crisis.

Moral Courage

Moral courage means having the inner strength, conviction, and fortitude to consciously exercise your free will toward goodness and virtue, regardless of the adverse consequences that might result from that decision. It means remaining true to your inner beliefs; engaging in behavior that demonstrates your principles, beliefs, and values; and not wavering in the face of unpopular sentiment, criticism, or direct pressure to behave otherwise. It often requires self-sacrifice and makes you vulnerable to others who will seek to discredit you for your ethical views.

Moral courage is the single most-important character trait you should cultivate and possess. All the other ethical values depend on it—it is the foundation upon which the others rest. If you have moral courage, all your other ethical values and virtues become real. Without it, you are left with noble but hollow platitudes.

I have observed a strange irony with respect to moral courage. Too often, a display of moral courage is frowned upon, discouraged, or heavily criticized. These negative consequences make it even more difficult for people to demonstrate personal moral courage. After all, if being a morally courageous person results in blame and insult, instead of praise, why would a reasonable person subject himself to such consequences?

Consider, for example, the executive who, upon discovering a widespread pattern of corporate misconduct within his organization, reports it to his superiors. When nothing is done to fix the inappropriate behavior, he goes public with the information. Ironically, the executive is not praised for his ethics, values, and integrity. Instead, he is branded a "whistleblower," referred to as a "snitch," characterized as a disloyal, disgruntled employee, and is black-listed from the industry. These responses have been experienced by many whistleblowers who have sought to correct unethical practices. After all, no one likes a snitch!

At the 1998 Winter Olympic Games in Nagano, Japan, the highly favored and touted United States Men's Hockey Team, made up of professional NHL players, failed to win a medal. The team's on-ice performance was deplorable. It was nothing, however, in comparison to the personal behavior of several team members who, after being eliminated from medal play, destroyed several rooms within the Olympic Village. The dollar cost of the damage was $3,000. Understandably, representatives from the United States Olympic Committee denounced the behavior, called for an investigation, and urged those responsible to identify themselves and pay for the damage. Curiously, not one member of the Men's Hockey Team came forward. Investigations by the National Hockey League yielded no indictments of who was responsible.

The President of the United States Olympic Committee, Bill Hybl, was adamant that a proper apology be made and that those involved be appropriately disciplined. The incident was widely reported in the press. In response to growing pressure from the United States Olympic Committee, Chris Chelios, the captain of the U.S. Men's Olympic Hockey Team, stepped forward and, without identifying the culprits, sent a letter of apology to the Japanese along with a check for $3,000 to cover the damage.

Incredibly, as news of this development broke, the owner of the Chicago Blackhawks, Bill Wirtz, circulated to the media a letter he had written criticizing Bill Hybl and the United States Olympic Committee for their efforts in seeking the apology. In his letter, Wirtz compared Hybl to Jonathan Swift, author of *Gulliver's Travels,* for blowing the incident out of proportion. He also compared him to Captain Queeg, the cowardly character who obsessed over stolen strawberries in the movie *The Caine Mutiny*.

I mention this incident for two reasons. First, although Chelios's apology and remittance of the $3,000 was a noble personal gesture, he lost an opportunity to demonstrate moral courage by identifying his teammates who had actually caused the damage. Second, the highly ethical stance of Hybl and the Olympic Committee should have been praised as courageous, not criticized. The criticism they endured from Wirtz illustrates my point that those who take morally courageous positions are often castigated and ridiculed.

After Chelios's letter, Richard Schultz, Executive Director of the United States Olympic Committee, was quoted as saying: "Obviously, I'd still hope the people responsible would have the courage to say, 'Hey, we were frustrated, upset, and we made a mistake.' " Odd isn't it? It really doesn't seem like such a hard thing to do. But at some inner personal level, a few professional hockey players who were given the chance to play in the Olympics can't seem to find what it takes to demonstrate the Olympic ideals of good sportsmanship. In this instance, moral courage was totally lacking in these individuals.

To be morally courageous requires great inner conviction that many are unable to find. These people will never achieve ethical virtuosity. Those who consistently demonstrate moral courage, however, will achieve ethical virtuosity.

I was once told a story about a police captain who received a phone call from the jail's evening shift commander. It seems that the captain's 17-year-old son had been drinking and was picked up by an officer for public intoxication. The youth was being detained at the jail, and the shift commander wanted to know what to do with the captain's son.

The captain loved his son deeply. This was the first instance of any trouble with the star student and athlete who was destined to go on to college on a scholarship. The captain knew that the conditions at the jail were harsh. He dreaded the thought of his beloved son being incarcerated, particularly when the other inmates would be aware that the boy was the son of a police captain. The jail's shift commander was a close personal friend, and would have done whatever the captain wanted. The captain was tempted by his emotions to ask that his son be released. After agonizing over it for several minutes, however, the captain asked the jail commander what would happen if his son had not been the child of a police captain. The jail commander told him that the boy would not be released, but would instead be detained and booked. The captain, with great pain in his heart, thanked the jail commander for his call, and told him to treat his son just like any other youth charged with the same crime.

Some people (I suspect most of whom are loving fathers) told me later that they believe the captain's decision was wrong, but they know at a deep personal level that this is what moral courage is all about.

Don't you agree that we need a lot more people like the police captain, and fewer people like the irresponsible players on the 1998 U.S. Men's Olympic Hockey Team?

Personal Accountability

In addition to cultivating moral courage, the sixth step toward ethical virtuosity requires that you hold yourself personally accountable for your own actions. We seem to be living in a time when personal accountability is overshadowed by attempts to evade the consequences of our decisions and behavior.

Lawsuits are burdening our courts because people are breaching their contracts, making defective products that maim people, engaging in deceptive and fraudulent business practices, and generally refusing to act in a responsible manner. The days of a verbal promise and a handshake have been replaced by voluminous pages of detailed contractual language specifying contingencies for every possibility. It seems rare to encounter a person whose word is sufficient and reliable.

I am reminded of a story told to me years ago by a law professor who was trying to explain the true nature of what it means to be a lawyer in our judicial system. The story goes like this:

Mrs. Jones owned a goat. It was a friendly goat, but like many goats, it preferred a variety of foods. Normally, Mrs. Jones kept her goat tied securely to a fence post so that it would not wander away and menace the neighbors.

Mrs. Smith lived next door to Mrs. Jones. Mrs. Smith loved flowers and spent most of her spring and summer months cultivating beautiful flowers, which were prized and valued by many of her friends. She was even beginning to make money off the sale of her flowers. Flowers, it seems, were her reason for existence.

One day, Mrs. Jones's goat gnawed through the rope that secured it to the fence post. The goat made its way to Mrs. Smith's treasured flower garden and proceeded to dine to its heart's content, virtually destroying all the seedlings, sprouts, and flowers Mrs. Smith had so diligently planted and cared for.

When Mrs. Smith discovered the goat standing in her garden with a few flowers hanging from its mouth, she became unraveled and attacked the goat with her fists. The goat managed a quick bite to her left leg. Enraged, Mrs. Smith picked up a hoe and chased the goat out of her garden. Fortunately for the goat, it managed to escape Mrs. Smith's wrath. Unfortunately for Mrs. Smith, however, she returned to her garden and slipped on a hose, breaking her hip, which required a total hip replacement. After her surgery, Mrs. Smith developed a serious life-threatening staph infection that resulted in the amputation of her left leg.

To say the least, Mrs. Smith was a bit peeved. She sued Mrs. Jones and her own surgeon, claiming that Mrs. Jones was responsible for her lost flowers, her amputated left leg from the goat bite, her hip replacement, emotional distress, and pain and suffering. She claimed that the surgeon was negligent in not properly treating the staph infection.

Mrs. Jones denied all responsibility for Mrs. Smith's condition. First, she claimed that her goat was the victim of a mistaken identity, and that it was not her goat that ate Mrs. Smith's flowers. Second, Mrs. Jones alleged that if it was indeed her goat that did the dastardly deed, her goat was not guilty by reason of insanity, caused by the traumatic separation it suffered when it was prematurely taken from its parents. Third, if it was her goat, her goat had been lost for several days, seeking refuge in another part of the city in order to escape the maniacal ravings of Mrs. Smith. Fourth, if it was her goat, it had become ill as a result of eating the toxic and hazardous flowers Mrs. Smith cultivated, suffering miserably and causing Mrs. Jones to incur substantial veterinary fees. Fifth, Mrs. Jones herself was suffering great emotional distress from the absence of her goat and its illness. Sixth, Mrs. Jones contended that any injuries Mrs. Smith might have suffered were caused to herself because she boxed with the goat and did not notice the location of her own garden hose. Not only did Mrs. Jones deny liability, but she countersued Mrs. Smith for her goat's losses and her own emotional distress.

The surgeon denied any liability to Mrs. Smith, saying it was the goat bite on Mrs. Smith's leg that caused the staph infection, and that he was a surgeon, not a bacteriologist. When Mrs. Smith's HMO failed to pay for the amputation (saying it had not been approved in advance), the surgeon sued Mrs. Smith for payment.

Mrs. Smith in turn sued her HMO for breach of contract. The HMO went bankrupt and did not bother to file a response.

This story is humorous, but it does serve to illustrate my point: We as a society have lost our sense of personal accountability. Having practiced law for a good many years, I can tell you that the denials, defenses, and attempts to escape personal liability that are offered up in most trials are as numerous, clever, and frivolous as the defenses of Mrs. Jones, the surgeon, and the HMO. In fact, lawyers are handsomely rewarded and held in high esteem when they successfully get their clients off the hook.

We need to return to a sense of individual personal accountability, where we hold ourselves accountable for our actions and step up and make right that which we have caused by our erroneous decisions and conduct. This is hard to do. I know this from personal experience.

I was in southern California nearing the end of a week-long business trip, and I was tired and in a hurry to get to the airport to make my flight home. I was in a rental car, driving along a freeway that I thought would take me directly to the Los Angeles airport. I was mistaken. When I finally realized my error, I stopped and asked for directions back to the airport. The convenience store clerk, who barely spoke English, muttered something about turning left at the second stop light. I was running out of time and running out of patience, and I was in an unfamiliar city. I knew I was lost. I really wanted to make that flight home.

When I came to the second stop light, I found myself in the right lane of a two-lane left turn. When I glanced down at the map to check my location, someone behind me tooted a horn. I looked up and saw that the light had changed to a green arrow pointing left. I proceeded to turn left, crossed the oncoming lane of traffic and was surprised to see that the ramp leading to the freeway had been barricaded off with small orange traffic cones. I was already committed, since I was now in the oncoming traffic lane. It seemed odd that these orange cones had been placed in such a way that a car could easily pass through them. Before I gave this any more thought, I saw out of my peripheral vision a car in the adjacent left lane pass between the orange cones in his lane. I didn't think much about it, and did the same. So did all the other cars behind me. I was about to accelerate and follow the first car to the freeway when to my surprise, a California highway patrol car came screaming down the up ramp directly toward us. To say the least, this officer was peeved. He had an attitude and I was the direct target of it. He blocked our path and ordered the other drivers and me to "freeze" with our hands on our steering wheels. This I did without hesitation. He came to my window and commanded me to give him my driver's license and car registration. I immediately complied.

While he returned to his car, I had visions of disappearing deep into the bowels of the California jail system. My mind raced over my circumstances. I knew I would miss my plane and I knew this was *not my fault!* After all, I was an out-of-state business traveler, lost in an unfamiliar city, and I was following directions given me by a foreigner. The light had turned green with an arrow indicating the left turn. I had an impatient driver behind me. I did not see the orange barrier cones until I was committed and positioned in the oncoming lanes of traffic. I had no other place to go than where I had gone. The barrier cones were wide enough for me to pass through. I simply followed a local driver through the cones, and other drivers did the same thing. I had all kinds of excuses for why I was not responsible.

I sat there for 20 minutes while the officer spoke to all the other drivers behind me. Each was allowed to go free. Finally, when he came to me, I could see he was still agitated. I was reminded of a speech I had just given on the need for emotional discipline and personal accountability. As much as I wanted to tell this officer how mistaken he was and how justified I was in my conduct, something told me that this was not the right thing to do. When he asked me why I had broken through the barrier, I mustered all the strength I had and explained in a quiet, humble voice that I was lost, I was trying to get to the airport, and I had made a mistake. This was incredibly difficult to do, given my underlying emotional condition. I cringed as this officer lectured me for five minutes, telling me that I had violated California law and caused a mild traffic jam, and that I should be better prepared the next time I came to California. This, too, was difficult to take. But something deep within me told me to simply be quiet. I made a mistake and I needed to hold myself accountable. When the officer finished his tirade, he looked at me, shook his head, and said, "Okay, since you realized your mistake, admitted it, and didn't give me any lip, I'm going to let you off on this violation." I thanked him and cautiously pulled away, grateful for his benevolent exercise of discretion in my favor. I often wonder what the result would have been if I had given in to my emotions and tried to rationalize and justify my behavior. I was grateful that in this instance, I had listened to my own talk and was prepared to hold myself accountable for my own actions.

How often do *you* demonstrate personal accountability? To what extent do you acknowledge your errors and remedy the wrong you have caused, even when you feel that you were justified? Is personal accountability something that others believe you possess?

A friend of mine once told me about an individual who had just been hired as an office manager. She was responsible for submitting a variety of forms to the central corporate headquarters in order to get the payroll to the employees on time, but was still somewhat unfamiliar with the procedures of her new employer. The office manager did what she was supposed to do and the payroll checks arrived on time—that is, all but one. It seems that one of the clerks did not receive a check. This was not the first time this particular clerk had been the victim of a central-headquarters payroll mistake. She told the office manager of the error and how headquarters was always screwing up the payroll.

The office manager made a few inquires and discovered that headquarters had not erred, but *she* had when she prepared the forms. The office manager undertook the steps to submit the proper forms, but she was told that the payroll check would not arrive for ten days. She knew that no one would know that the mistake was hers. She thought about what she was going to say to the clerk and to the other employees who wanted to blame headquarters for the error. She could have lied and no one would have ever known. Her image and reputation would have remained intact.

Instead, the office manager confessed her mistake to the clerk and wrote her a personal check to cover the clerk's need for funds, pending the arrival of the payroll check in ten days.

This conduct represents to me the epitome of personal accountability. The office manager was under no obligation to place her own funds at risk. She could have lied and successfully avoided all blame for the mistake. She acknowledged her error, however, and made it right. I wonder how many of us would have done the same thing. Would you have responded in such an ethical manner?

Reflections

Think back for a moment and reflect on the concepts of moral courage and personal accountability. What do they mean to you? Are they relevant in your life? Have you missed opportunities to demonstrate moral courage and personal accountability? Do you now face a situation that calls for moral courage and personal accountability? How will you respond?

*You have to make
a behavioral commitment.*

You have to have a plan
and follow it daily.

19

Step 7: Develop an Action Plan

The seventh step toward ethical virtuosity requires you to make a commitment. It involves developing and following an individual plan of action. The first six steps are really quite simple to know and understand. The real challenge is personally following through and demonstrating these ethical principles in your daily personal and business conduct.

Your subordinates, co-workers, family, and friends look to you for leadership and inspiration. Are you prepared and willing to meet this ethical challenge? Can you say without hesitation that you will make a personal commitment to follow the seven steps to ethical virtuosity?

It is not too late for you to accept the ethical challenge and make a significant statement to move yourself toward authentic virtue and genuine goodness. If you make a genuine commitment to achieve ethical virtuosity, you will be rewarded in many ways.

The choice is uniquely and individually yours. What type of ethical legacy will you leave behind for others? Will your footprints lead them to ethics, integrity, and good moral character?

Do you have the genuine desire to achieve ethical virtuosity? How many dimensions of ethical virtuosity do you now possess? Do you truly know yourself? Do you seek ethical knowledge on a regular basis? Have you developed a personal ethical belief system that is uniquely your own? Do you exercise emotional discipline when confronted with ethical dilemmas? Do you truly and consciously exercise your free will so that goodness and virtue result? Are you morally courageous, and do you consistently demonstrate personal accountability?

Finally, are you willing to make a commitment and develop your individual response to the ethics challenge by developing a personal plan of action?

• • • • •

Bibliography

Andrews, K. R. (1989). *Ethics in practice: Managing the moral corporation.* Boston: Harvard Business School Press.

Audi, R. (ed.). (1995). *The Cambridge dictionary of philosophy.* Cambridge: Cambridge University Press.

Badaracco, J. L. (1989). *Defining moments.* Boston: Harvard Business School Press.

Badaracco, J. L., and Ellsworth, R. R. (1989). *Leadership and the quest for integrity.* Boston: Harvard Business School Press.

Becker, L. (ed.). (1992). *Encyclopedia of ethics.* New York: Garland Publishing.

Casey, J. L. (1989). *Ethics in the financial marketplace.* New York: Scudder, Stevens, and Clark.

Dosick, W. (1993). *The business bible.* New York: William Morrow.

Edwards, P. (ed.). (1967). *The encyclopedia of philosophy.* New York: Macmillan Company.

Goleman, D. (1995). *Emotional intelligence.* New York: Bantam Books.

Kelly, C. M. (1988). *The destructive achiever: Power and ethics in the American corporation.* Reading, Massachusetts: Addison-Wesley.

Kidder, R. M. (1995). *How good people make tough choices.* New York: William Morrow and Company, Inc.

Larimer, L. V. (1996). *The ethical type indicator.* Colorado Springs, Colorado: The Larimer Center for Ethical Leadership.

MacIntyre, A. (1966). *A short history of ethics.* New York: Macmillan Publishing.

Madsen, P., and Shafritz, J. (eds.) (1990). *The essentials of business ethics.* New York: Meridian.

McGreal, I. (ed.). (1992). *Great thinkers of the western world.* New York: HarperCollins.

Nash, L. L. (1993). *Good intentions aside.* Boston: Harvard Business School Press.

Seilbert, D., and Proctor, W. (1984). *The ethical executive.* New York: Cornerstone Library.

Solomon, R. C., and Hanson, K. (1985). *It's good business.* New York: Atheneum.

The business roundtable statement on corporate responsibility. (1982, January). New York: The Business Roundtable.

Thomason, J. (1986). *The ethics of Aristotle: The Nicomachean ethics.* Great Britain: Penguin Books.

Thoughts on virtue. (1996). Chicago: Triumph Books.

Toffler, B. (1986). *Tough choices: Managers talk ethics.* New York: John Wiley.

Weiss, L. (1998). *What is the emperor wearing? Truth telling in business relationships.* Boston: Butterworth-Heinemann.

••••• |

About Focused Strategies, Inc.

Focused Strategies' mission is to help leaders promote, inspire, and encourage ethics, integrity, and responsible business conduct within their organizations so that the devastating consequences of internal fraud, scandal, corruption, and litigation are avoided.

This mission is fulfilled by offering ethics training, ethics curriculum development, ethical leadership seminars, integrity-based leadership seminars, motivational conference keynotes and speeches on ethics and integrity, publications on ethics and integrity, ethics and compliance program planning, assistance developing codes of conduct, ethics assessments, and ethics investigations.

Ethics Training

Focused Strategies, Inc., has developed a series of highly effective, inspirational, and pragmatic ethics training curriculums. These include the following:

- Integrity-Based-Leadership: 12 Steps That Promote, Inspire, and Encourage Ethics, Integrity, and Responsible Business Conduct
- Ethical Virtuosity: Seven Strategies to Help Leaders Do the Right Thing at the Right Time
- Understanding Your Ethical Type

- Ethical Leadership: Leadership Principles and Techniques That Work

- Identifying and Promoting Core Organizational Values

- Ethical but Effective Negotiation Techniques, Skills, and Strategies

Keynote and Conference Speeches

Louie V. Larimer, President of Focused Strategies, Inc., is an accomplished motivational speaker who restores ethical visions, rekindles ethical passions, and inspires integrity.

He is a member of the National Speakers Association, and speaks all across the United States at major conventions and corporate meetings.

His speeches are substantive, entertaining, inspiring, and laced with practical insights, substantive knowledge, and down-to-earth humor. His repertoire includes:

- Leading with Integrity: 12 Ways to Promote, Inspire, and Encourage Ethics, Integrity, and Responsible Business Conduct

- Ethical Virtuosity: Seven Strategies to Help You Do the Right Thing at the Right Time

- Identifying Your Ethical Type: Seven Ways of Resolving Ethical Dilemmas

- Ethical Myths: Why Good People Do Stupid Things

- How to Make Ethics, Integrity, and Character Meaningful and Relevant in Your Personal and Business Life

Integrity-Based Leadership

There is an urgent need for leaders of business, industry, and government to promote, inspire, and encourage ethical behavior and responsible decisions. This is a difficult and complex challenge that many leaders do not know how to meet. Few, if any, have had significant, relevant, and practical ethics training.

When confronted with ethical or moral dilemmas, some leaders choose to ignore the ethical implications, while others deliberately act irresponsibly.

The consequences of such decisions and conduct are devastating. They include multimillion dollar judgments, bankruptcy, outrageous attorney fees, loss of public confidence, public humiliation, decline in employee morale, loss of customer loyalty, tarnished images, and destroyed careers.

It doesn't have to be that way.

The Integrity-Based Leadership Training Module was specifically designed to give leaders and managers of complex organizations the practical knowledge and skills that will enable them to foster sound ethical decisions and responsible conduct within their organizational units.

The Integrity-Based Leadership Module is suitable for first-line supervisors and above. It provides a foundation for understanding one's own ethical constitution and core ethical values. It presents a disciplined process of critical thinking and reflective judgment, and introduces participants to a variety of fundamental ethical concepts and analytical principles. This results in the development of a behavior-specific plan of action that will promote, inspire, and encourage ethics, integrity, and responsible business conduct within their departments.

The highlight of the program is the use of *The Ethical Type Indicator*, a personal assessment instrument that identifies the primary ethical preference of each participant. In addition, participants are taught how to identify their core ethical values and engage in a formalized process of reflective thought.

The Ethical Type Indicator

How do you resolve the moral and ethical dilemmas that arise in your life? Can you identify, articulate, and defend the ethical principles that guide your decisions and conduct? Do you know your ethical type?

If you teach ethics, have you found a meaningful way to help your students answer the above inquiries? If you are a parent, have you found an effective tool that will help you instill conscious choices and reflective judgment skills in your children? If you are a corporate trainer, are you looking for a new, exciting, and highly effective ethics training tool that will promote, inspire, and encourage ethics, integrity, and responsible business conduct?

The Ethical Type Indicator is a personal assessment instrument that measures the extent to which a person uses seven ethical preferences when confronted with an ethical dilemma.

The instrument consists of 42 statements or affirmations. Each statement is reflective of one of the seven different ethical preferences. The participant reads each statement and indicates the extent to which he or she agrees or disagrees with the statement.

The instrument is self-scoring and provides each participant with an individual profile of his or her ethical type and ethical preferences. The results allow and encourage individual self-discovery and self-exploration.

The instrument is also available in a format for third-party input so that participants can compare ethical type self-ratings with the perceptions of others who rate how they believe the participants resolve ethical dilemmas. This version is a powerful and insightful tool that is being used in the United States Office of Personnel Management's Western Development Leadership Center programs.

Corporate trainers should take note that *The Ethical Type Indicator* is best used within the context of *The Ethical Type Indicator Training Manual.*

This training manual outlines how to use the instrument in two-hour, half-day, and full-day formats. The manual is embodied in a trainer's guide that includes specific instructions, scripts, overhead slide masters, and interactive exercises—everything you need to conduct your own in-house training program.

Ethics Assessments

The ultimate success of any ethics and compliance program depends on the breadth, depth, and quality of the initial ethics assessment of the organization. The Larimer Center helps leaders conduct comprehensive self-assessments of their operating environments that identify corporate business practices that unnecessarily expose the organization to liability and result in fraud, scandal, corruption, and litigation. We do this in three ways:

- Personal interviews with members of your senior executive team to obtain perceptions concerning troublesome business practices they believe will ultimately result in some form of public embarrassment or litigation.

- Employee focus groups to solicit employee perceptions of practices that unnecessarily expose the organization to liability and public humiliation.

- Administration of The Litigation Prevention Inventory, an assessment instrument that identifies the organization's vulnerability to 60 common forms of corporate and employee misconduct.

Ethics and Compliance Consultation

We will help you design, plan, and implement an effective ethics and compliance program that meets the requirements of the United States Corporate Sentencing Guidelines.

Under this federal statute, organizations that have established effective programs of ethics and compliance are entitled to mitigation credit and the reduction of potential fines and penalties resulting from corporate and employee violations of federal law.

We have identified national benchmarks and the best ethics and compliance practices, which we will share with you as you plan your initiative.

The best ethical practices are organized under 17 major focus areas. We will help you look at your current practices in relation to these national-best ethics and compliance practices and then assist you in planning, developing, and implementing your own unique ethics program.

Additional Information

To receive additional information, samples, or demonstration videos, or to order books, contact us at the following address:

Focused Strategies, Inc.
524 South Cascade Avenue, Suite 1
Colorado Springs, Colorado 80903
(719) 636-8983